CULTURE SMART!
TRINIDAD AND TOBAGO

Tim Ewbank

·K·U·P·E·R·A·R·D·

ISBN 978 1 85733 543 9
This book is also available as an e-book: eISBN 978 1 85733 547 7

British Library Cataloguing in Publication Data
A CIP catalogue entry for this book is available from the British Library

First published in Great Britain 2011
by Kuperard, an imprint of Bravo Ltd
59 Hutton Grove, London N12 8DS
Tel: +44 (0) 20 8446 2440 Fax: +44 (0) 20 8446 2441
www.culturesmart.co.uk
Inquiries: sales@kuperard.co.uk

Distributed in the United States and Canada
by Random House Distribution Services
1745 Broadway, New York, NY 10019
Tel: +1 (212) 572-2844 Fax: +1 (212) 572-4961
Inquiries: csorders@randomhouse.com

Series Editor Geoffrey Chesler
Design Bobby Birchall

Printed in Malaysia

Cover image: *Carnival mask, Trinidad* © iStockphoto.com

Images on the following pages by kind permission of Carole Anne Ferris at www.cafemokagallery.com: 12, 13, 16 (left and right), 30 (top and bottom), 31, 35, 36, 43, 44, 46, 47, 48, 49, 50, 51, 52, 56, 58, 67 (bottom), 69 (bottom), 71, 74 (top and bottom), 75, 76, 79, 81, 83, 88, 98, 100, 102, 103, 104, 115, 116, 117, 121 (bottom), and 146

Images on the following pages reproduced under Creative Commons Attribution Share-Alike Unported 3.0 license: 84 © Kalamazadkhan; 93 © Ukexpat; 101 © Pymouss; and 111 © Belchman 9006

Images on these pages reproduced under Creative Commons Attribution 2.0 Generic license: 93 (top) © Dominic Sayers; 95 © Jimmy Harris; and 164 © cheesy42

On page 32 Creative Commons Attribution 2.5 Brazil license © Antonio Cruz; on page 89 Creative Commons Attribution 2.0 Germany license © Reinhard Jahn; and on page 145 GNU Free Documentation License © Chris Fitzpatrick

About the Author

TIM EWBANK was born in Bournemouth, England. He started his career in journalism after graduating from Aberdeen University, where he gained a distinction in English. He has worked for several English national newspapers, including the *Daily Mail*, covering assignments all over the world. Tim is the author of sixteen books, including best-selling biographies of footballer David Beckham, cricketer Andrew Flintoff, and singer Rod Stewart. As a travel writer he has worked in TV and radio, and contributed articles to a wide range of international newspapers and magazines. For the past sixteen years he has been a regular visitor to Trinidad and Tobago, where his partner has a home in Port of Spain.

The Culture Smart! series is continuing to expand. For further information and latest titles visit **www.culturesmart.co.uk**

The publishers would like to thank **CultureSmart!**Consulting for its help in researching and developing the concept for this series.

CultureSmart!Consulting creates tailor-made seminars and consultancy programs to meet a wide range of corporate, public-sector, and individual needs. Whether delivering courses on multicultural team building in the USA, preparing Chinese engineers for a posting in Europe, training call-center staff in India, or raising the awareness of police forces to the needs of diverse ethnic communities, it provides essential, practical, and powerful skills worldwide to an increasingly international workforce.

For details, visit www.culturesmartconsulting.com

CultureSmart!Consulting and **CultureSmart!** guides have both contributed to and featured regularly in the weekly travel program "Fast Track" on BBC World TV.

contents

contents

Map of Trinidad and Tobago

introduction

introduction

The first thing to know about Trinidad and Tobago is that the two islands could hardly be more different. For most people, the Caribbean conjures up images of a poster-perfect paradise, sun-kissed beaches, palm trees swaying in the warm breeze, and the tinkling of steelpan music never far away. But while this preconception largely holds true for Tobago, Trinidad has too much going on to bother unduly with tourism.

With bustling, hectic Port of Spain as its capital, Trinidad is cosmopolitan, culturally diverse, and multiethnic. A population descended from East Indian, African, Spanish, French, Dutch, American, Chinese, Syrian, and English forebears gets along in relative harmony. High-rise towers, old colonial-style houses, and gothic cathedrals somehow blend with Hindu mandirs, flagship hotels, Muslim mosques, modern apartment complexes, and newly built houses displaying Hindu prayer flags. It's a potent population mix with an underlying vibrancy that explodes into full expression each February with the celebration of Carnival—a dazzling, open-to-all-comers, mass participation street extravaganza of steel bands, calypso, dance, and the magnificent spectacle of the imaginatively and colorfully costumed bands "playing mas" (short for masquerade). Not for nothing is Trinidad known as the party island.

By contrast, Trinidad's sister island Tobago is much quieter, predominantly rural, heavily forested and, aside from its busy capital, Scarborough, and a handful of other small towns and villages, its charm lies in its picturesque bays and unspoiled beaches, although, to cater to its burgeoning tourism, hotels and resorts are gradually laying claim to stretches of its coastline.

Trinis, as Trinidadians like to be called, are by nature friendly, outgoing, laid-back, and hospitable and need no second invitation to enjoy themselves, usually to a Caribbean beat. They have a history of slavery and indentured labor that, even today, engenders a determination to live their lives as they choose rather than to order. They know their country has problems and want these addressed with common sense, which, they believe, is all too often lacking at the top.

This book explores the codes and paradoxes of Trinbagonian life, mindful of its many and varied traditions, customs, and cultures. It outlines the islands' contrasting histories and opens a window into people's private lives, showing how they interact socially, and their attitudes to visitors who are "from foreign." It offers practical advice from how to play mas at Carnival to how to meet and make friends. *Culture Smart! Trinidad and Tobago* sets out to take you beyond the clichés to connect with the real people.

Key Facts

Official Name	Republic of Trinidad and Tobago	
Capital City	Port of Spain (Trinidad)	Scarborough (Tobago)
Main Cities/Towns	Trinidad: Chaguanas, Arima, San Fernando	Tobago: Roxborough, Charlotteville, Plymouth
Population	Total T&T 1,229,953 (Tobago 55,000)	
Ethnic Makeup	East Indian 40.3%; African 39.6%; mixed race Caribs 18%; Chinese 1.2%; Lebanese, Syrian	
Age Structure	0–14 years: 19.6% 15–64 years: 72.6% 65 years and over: 7.9%	
Area	Trinidad: 1,864 sq. miles (4,828 sq. km)	Tobago: 116 sq. miles (300 sq. km)
Geography	The two islands lie in the Caribbean Sea off the northeast coast of Venezuela, which is 7 miles (11 km) away from Trinidad.	Tobago is 20 miles (32 km) from Trinidad.
Terrain	Trinidad has three mountain ranges, valleys, and rolling plains.	Tobago is mountainous and heavily forested with hardwood trees.
Climate	Tropical: no summer or winter, only wet and dry seasons. Not in the usual path of Atlantic hurricanes	

Natural Resources	Oil and natural gas make up 80% of exports.	The rest are primarily rice, coffee, cocoa, citrus fruits, bananas, and fish.
Currency	Trinidad & Tobago dollar ($TT)	
Language	Officially English	Also Caribbean Hindustani, French, Spanish, Chinese
Religion	Catholic 32%; Protestant 28%; Hindu 24%	Minority faiths: Anglican, Baptist, Pentecostal, Muslim, Seventh-day Adventist, and other Christian denominations
Government	T&T is a republic and a parliamentary democracy.	The president is head of state elected for a five-year term.
Media	Three of nine TV channels are government-owned. Cable TV is widely available.	Three main daily newspapers, but just one in Tobago
Electricity	Mostly 110 volts	220 volts for some appliances like air-conditioning and ovens
DVD/Video	NTSC Area 4	Many DVDs multiregional now
Internet Domain	.tt	
Telephone	T&T's country code is 001868.	Dial 1 out to USA, Canada, Caribbean. To elsewhere, dial 011 and then the country code.
Time Zone	GMT-4 hours	

chapter one

LAND &
PEOPLE

GEOGRAPHY

The Republic of Trinidad and Tobago consists of two main islands, and several islets, totaling 1,980 square miles (5,128 sq. km). They form the southernmost islands of the Lesser Antilles chain and lie in the Caribbean Sea, with Trinidad, once part of the South American mainland, situated 6.8 miles (11 km) off the northeast coast of Venezuela.

Roughly rectangular in shape with three projecting peninsular corners, Trinidad is by far the larger of the two main islands at 1,864 sq. miles (4,828 sq. km) and is within sight of the Venezuelan coast, separated by the Gulf of Paria.

Tobago lies 20 miles (32 km) northeast of Trinidad and totals 116 square miles (300 sq. km). It has several small satellite islands.

Trinidad and Tobago are surrounded by the tranquil Caribbean Sea on their north coasts and by the less calm Atlantic Ocean on their southern and eastern sides. Geologically and biologically they are part of continental South America but they are very different due to centuries of separation.

Three mountain ranges cross Trinidad. The rain-forested Northern Range traverses and

dominates the northern part of the island, reaching a height of 3,100 feet (945 m) at Mount Aripo. To the north of the range are Trinidad's most popular beaches—Maracas Bay, Las Cuevas, and Blanchisseuse, with miles of unspoiled coastline. The Central Range crosses the island diagonally, rising to a height of 1,066 feet (325 m), below which are agricultural flatlands and the central plains. The Southern Range rises to a maximum of 1,001 feet (305 m); aside from Trinidad's second city, San Fernando, the south of the island is the least populated.

Tropical forests cover half of the island and swamps are found along parts of the east and west coasts. There are numerous rivers and streams but they are short. The longest river is the Ortoire in Trinidad, between Nariva and Mayaro, stretching 31 miles (50 km) eastward to the Atlantic Ocean in the south.

No less than 60 percent of Tobago is covered with forest; the island is hilly and dominated by the Main Ridge Forest Reserve, which is 18 miles (29 km) long with its summit Pigeon Peak at 1,860 feet (549 m) above sea level. There are valleys to both the north and south of the Main Ridge. Scarborough is the only major port in Tobago but several small harbors and dozens of unspoiled bays, inlets, and sheltered sandy beaches indent Tobago's coastline.

CLIMATE

Closer to the Equator than any other islands in the Caribbean, Trinidad and Tobago have the benefit of a tropical climate all year-round, with the temperature varying only very slightly. Moderated by the constant northeast trade winds, the maximum temperature averages 89°F (32°C) during the day and 72°F (22°C) at night. The mean temperature is 85°F (29°C) with 60 percent humidity. Foreigners can find the 75 percent humidity oppressive from June to December, but Tobago tends to be slightly cooler and less humid because it catches more of the breeze from the trade winds.

The sister islands have two distinct seasons—
the wet season from June to November, and the
dry season from January to May, but it is hottest
between June and October. The dry season does
not mean drought because in most areas rain falls
every few days. Nighttime temperatures can drop
to around 70°F (21°C) in the cooler months.
Although Tobago can be wet at various times
during May, June, and July, the difference between
the two seasons is much less marked than on
Trinidad. The two islands experience around
40 inches (200 cm) of rainfall annually. Although
showers can be heavy, they usually last no longer
than two hours before brilliant sunshine and
blue skies return.

Both islands are situated below the hurricane
belt and Trinidad always seems to be missed by
hurricanes. Tobago has been less fortunate and
was badly struck by Hurricane Flora in 1963,
which destroyed 2,750 of Tobago's 7,500 houses
as well as forcibly changing the face of Tobago's
economy. Banana, coconut, and cocoa plantations,
which largely sustained the economy, were
devastated and the damage led to the avoidance
of cash crop agriculture and more attention on
tourism. Hurricane Flora also devastated Tobago's
rain forest. Clumps of old-growth trees survived
but the mighty winds and the driving rainfall
ravaged 75 percent of the forest. Since then,
regeneration has occurred in a natural way.

Tobago felt some of the force of Hurricane Ivan
in 2004. It downed trees, caused power outages to
30 percent of the island, and forty-five homes lost

their roofs. Waves were estimated to reach 65 feet
(20 m). Ivan left twenty people homeless, and a
pregnant woman was killed by a falling tree. In all
Ivan impacted more than 1,000 people in Tobago,
but the damage was slight compared with the
devastation it went on to cause to neighboring
Grenada. In general, however, T&T experiences
less storm activity than some of the other islands
in the Caribbean.

THE PEOPLE

Trinidad and Tobago has one of the most ethnically
diverse populations in the Caribbean. According to
the most recent government census, 40.3 percent of
the people are of "East Indian" descent. The "East
Indians" are descended from indentured laborers
brought to Trinidad in the second half of the

nineteenth century to work on the sugar plantations.
Some 39.5 percent define themselves as of African
descent, while 18.4 percent are classified as "mixed."
There are significant communities of Chinese,
Middle Eastern, Portuguese, and people of other

European descent. The East Indian population tends to be more evenly distributed throughout rural areas, while the African-descended population is more urban in character. In Trinidad, about one-half of the population lives in an urbanized east–west corridor stretching from Diego Martin in the west to Arima in the east. In Tobago, the population is approximately 54,000 and 90 percent are of African origin, with a minority East Indian presence and resident expatriates.

A BRIEF HISTORY OF TRINIDAD
First Encounters

Christopher Columbus discovered Trinidad on his third voyage of exploration, on Tuesday July 31, 1498. He wrote enthusiastically to the King and Queen of Spain: "There we saw houses and people and very fair lands, lands as beautiful and green as the gardens of Valencia in the month of March."

Columbus first set foot on the island's south coast at Moruga, where the earliest Trinidadians, indigenous communities of Arawaks, lived in primitive thatched huts. The initial hostility he and his men encountered from the natives soon evaporated and prompted his sailors to form the eventual opinion that these were the friendliest people in the Caribbean. Fittingly, more than five hundred years on, visitors today still enthuse about Trinidad's green and beautiful lands and rate its inhabitants as extremely friendly.

It's believed that Columbus named the island La Trinidad after the three peaks of the Trinity Hills he had seen from his ship off the southern coast of the island. But there is a school of thought that he named the island after the Holy Trinity in grateful thanks for Providence, because at the point he reached it all his food had rotted and he was down to his last container of water.

While Columbus is given credit for literally putting Trinidad on the map, ancient artifacts in south Trinidad point to Amerindians inhabiting the island some five thousand years before his arrival. Although of indeterminate origin, it's safe to assume these early settlers came from South America and were fishermen and farmers.

Despite Trinidad's discovery by Columbus, it would take nearly a century before Spain established

the first European community there. After Columbus, Spain largely forgot about the island for more than thirty years and only started taking an interest in it again because of renewed European fascination with the legend of El Dorado—the idea that there was a "gilded" king living in a South American city whose streets were made of gold. For Europeans, Trinidad was an island en route to this mythical land of golden riches. Spain therefore deemed it worth preserving as a Spanish domain and, although it took a long time, colonization ultimately followed.

Colonization by Spain

Several settlements were attempted over the
next sixty years, starting in 1532, but they were
unsuccessful—each time the would-be colonists
were driven out by the now disenchanted
Amerindians. The year 1592 saw the arrival of
the first permanent settlers from Spain, led
by an El Dorado fortune hunter, Antonio de
Berrio. He instigated the building of a small town
called San Jose de Oruna, which included a jail,
a church, a town hall, and a governor's residence,
with the community under the authority of a
Cabildo, a governing body with wide executive
powers elected from among De Berrio's people.
San Jose, in the north of Trinidad, is now called
St. Joseph.

The Cabildo lasted until 1840, but the
intervening years were riven with attempts by the
British, the French, and the Dutch to seize control
of the burgeoning colony. Trinidad's inhabitants
also had to contend with constant raiding by
pirates. Neither did Spain give much backing to
San Jose in terms of money and resources. It
showed no great commitment to develop the area
and paid scant regard to the need to protect the
town and its people. The annual arrival of a single
ship from Seville to check on San Jose's progress
was the only real token of interest.

Left vulnerable and militarily exposed, in 1595
San Jose was sacked and burned by the English
courtier and explorer Sir Walter Raleigh. The
entire region was easy prey for Raleigh when he
joined the search for El Dorado along the

Orinoco River in what is now Venezuela. To add insult to injury, the English adventurer even had the impudence to take the governor of Trinidad away with him as a captive.

In time the town was rebuilt, but such was Spain's lack of interest that at times the Spanish population fell to no more than a hundred and fifty. It wasn't until 1687 that Spain started to take a little more interest in Trinidad by despatching Capuchin monks to the island to set up a number of missions in a bid to convert the Amerindians to Christianity.

This evolved into a form of semi-slavery, with the monks joining up with the Spanish planters to force the Amerindians into not only building churches but also working on the lucrative cocoa and tobacco plantations. Resentment of this enforcement among the indigenous inhabitants resulted in an uprising in 1699, in which three priests were murdered in San Rafael. Revenge was swift and led to the slaughter by Spanish soldiers of many hundreds of Amerindians in a massacre at Arena. Hundreds more fled inland and, over the years, as European settlers brought diseases to Trinidad from Europe to which the natives had no resistance, the indigenous population was effectively wiped out.

While Spain continued to show little desire to develop Trinidad, poverty among the settlers became so prevalent that in 1740 local leaders were moved to write to the King protesting that they were able to go to mass only once a year, and only when they borrowed clothes from each other.

As Spain found few of its own citizens willing to settle there, the King issued two important decrees, in 1777 and in 1783, which were to change the nature of the island's population. He offered French planters the chance to move to Trinidad from French islands in the West Indies, such as Guadaloupe and Martinique, on condition that they were Roman Catholic. Later he also encouraged settlers from France itself, where the populace was restless in the run-up to the Revolution of 1789.

Spain's invitations were eagerly accepted by many thousands. They arrived in such numbers in Trinidad, bringing their slaves with them, that by 1787 the population had increased tenfold to ten thousand. With them they also brought French traditions and their language, which changed the local culture and created a French patois. Land was apportioned to these new immigrants according to the number of slaves they brought with them, and to oversee this policy Spain installed in 1794 what turned out to be the last of Trinidad's Spanish governors, Don Jose Maria Chacon. He successfully put so much effort into the colony's economic and social growth that by the end of his administration in 1797 Trinidad had become one of the wealthiest islands in the West Indies.

British Rule

While the island flourished, it nevertheless remained virtually defenseless, and in February 1797 Spain paid for its neglect. A British fleet of eighteen ships, bearing seven thousand men under the command of Sir Ralph Abercromby, captured the island with barely a shot fired in retaliation. The defending force of five ships and just two thousand men was no match for the English and the commander of the Spanish fleet, Rear-Admiral Ruiz Apodoca, surrendered by scuttling his ships in Chaguaramas Bay. This humiliating submission saw Governor Chacon return to Spain in disgrace, and Trinidad, as well as Tobago, was to remain in British hands for the next hundred and sixty-five years, until the islands gained independence in 1962. Trinidad became a Crown Colony, governed according to Spanish and French laws but with all the key decisions made in London.

Abercromby's appointment of Thomas Picton as governor proved to be a chilling choice. A ruthless military man, he embarked on a reign of terror. Those suspected of being subversives were subjected to beatings, torture, and invariably met a hideous end by mutilation or hanging. Others were simply burned to death, and many more were summarily deported.

Slaves especially were subjected to appalling treatment and it is estimated that up to one-third of them perished while clearing the rain forests to make way for more plantations.

Trinidad suffered five years of Picton's bloodthirsty rule before he was removed, partly because his ironfisted methods were by now glaringly at odds with the antislavery movement gathering steam back in England. It was another five years before Britain abolished the slave trade, in 1807, and when the abolition of slavery followed in 1834, Trinidad found itself lacking the manpower to sustain the sugar industry, which had grown enormously over the past few decades. Freed slaves from other Caribbean islands partly helped to rectify the labor shortage, but the British government also authorized an indenture system for immigrants from India.

Indentured Labor

May 1845 saw the arrival of the first 225 laborers from Calcutta on board the *Fatel Rozack*. It heralded a mass migration from what is today India and Pakistan, which saw 145,000 arrive before the indentured labor scheme was stopped in 1917. Many thousands were permitted to return to India, as stipulated in their contracts, but the majority opted to remain and take advantage of the 5 acres (2 ha) of land they were entitled to at the end of their five-year indenture period. They were known as East Indians, to distinguish them from West Indians.

In truth, the conditions under which the mainly Muslim and Hindu indentured labor force worked and lived were little better than those experienced by the slaves. They worked a seven and a half hour day six days a week for five years at a rate of around 13 cents a day. In addition, the East Indians were viewed with contempt by Afro-Caribbeans because they regarded them as slaves to the white planters in all but name. In 1853, the first Chinese immigrants arrived in Trinidad to further swell the labor force.

Union with Tobago
In 1889 Trinidad and Tobago were amalgamated as a single British colony. Inevitably there was simmering resentment among Trinidadians that the island was being governed from London, and on several occasions during the years of British rule local anger turned into violence, most notably in 1903. A protest meeting held at Woodford Square in Port of Spain turned into an ugly riot resulting in the destruction by fire of the Red House, the seat of government, and the death of eighteen people shot by police.

It was not until 1913 that Joseph Chamberlain, Britain's Secretary of State for the Colonies, sanctioned an elected assembly for Trinidad and Tobago, but it was another twelve years before the first elections to the Legislative Council were held in 1925. The 1930s saw the rise of the trade union movement in Trinidad, and in the next two decades political parties emerged linked to the trade unions.

Independence and Political Unrest

In 1956 the People's National Movement (PNM) was founded by Eric Williams. In 1958–62, the islands were incorporated into the West Indies Federation. The desire for representative government, which had been present for so long, now increased dramatically and, on August 31, 1962, Trinidad and Tobago achieved full independence within the British Commonwealth, with Williams as prime minister.

In 1970 the Black Power movement spread to Trinidad and Tobago with the establishment of the National Joint Action Committee (NJAC), a party seeking fundamental changes in society after a survey found that 86 percent of business leaders were white. Williams faced a major political crisis from NJAC protest marches, during which a supporter was shot by police, and from strikes. When Williams declared a state of emergency, a small group of officers and men in the Trinidad and Tobago Defense Force seized control of the barracks at Teteron in sympathy with the protestors, thereby depriving the government of arms. Williams was forced to purchase arms from the USA and Venezuela and, once rearmed, the rest of the Defense Force remained loyal to the government with the support of the people. The crisis was averted when a series of planned strikes were called off.

On August 1, 1976, the country became a republic, with the former governor general Ellis Clarke as president and Williams as prime minister. The 1986 general elections saw the emergence of a new coalition under the banner of the Tobago-based National Alliance for Reconstruction. The party achieved an historic victory, resoundingly defeating the PNM after thirty years in power.

In 1990 members of an extreme Islamic minority group, the Jamaat al Muslimeen, stormed parliament and took the prime minister and his cabinet hostage in a rebellion that killed twenty-four people. The rebels eventually surrendered and were later pardoned. The group's leader, Yasin Abu Bakr, blamed the government for the widespread poverty that followed the collapse of world oil prices.

A BRIEF HISTORY OF TOBAGO

Although Christopher Columbus landed in Trinidad in 1498, he merely sighted the island of Tobago in the distance, named it Bella Forma (beautifully formed), and sailed on. The island's name Tobago is almost certainly a derivation from Tavaco, the word for the long pipe in which the original inhabitants burned and inhaled the smoke of tobacco, which they cultivated and which was subsequently grown by settlers as a crop. Tobago, which existed quite separately from Trinidad for centuries, can justifiably lay claim to being one of the most fought-over islands in the

world. The early Carib population were
constantly fighting off other Amerindian tribes,
long before the major European seafaring powers
regularly battled for control of the island in the
late sixteenth and seventeenth centuries.

Colonial Rivalry

British sailors were the first to lay claim to Tobago
by nailing a flag to a tree in 1580, but in 1632 the
Dutch founded a township near Scarborough,
complete with vast warehouses to store the sugar
for which the island was by then well-known.
Then, in 1641, King Charles I gave Tobago to his
godson, the Duke of Courland, as a birthday
present. It is thought that over the next two
hundred years control of the island changed
hands more than thirty times as the Spanish,
Dutch, English, French, and Courlanders
(Latvians) waged bitter battles to claim Tobago
for themselves. So intense was the battle for
supremacy among the European powers that in
1684 the Treaty of Aix La Chapelle ruled
that the island was to be a no-
man's-land in which people
from all nationalities should
be free to settle. This enabled
British, French, and Dutch
to live together relatively
harmoniously with free
Africans and Caribs, but it also
meant that Tobago became a
haven for pirates, including the
notorious Henry Morgan.

British Rule

In 1762, however, the all-comers policy was brushed aside when the English captured Tobago, and the Treaty of Paris the following year ceded the island to Britain with the land duly divided up into parishes and sold off. A permanent settlement was founded at Georgetown and, as more English and Scots arrived with their slaves, the island's cotton, indigo, and sugar estates flourished. Within a decade more than three thousand African slaves were working under fewer than three hundred white overseers as the island became a British sugar colony.

The French returned to the island and twice seized control, from 1781 to 1793 and from 1801 to 1802. During the latter period, the island's citizens actually went to the polls and elected Napoleon Bonaparte First Consul of the Republic for life.

In the following years, 1803–14, the British again wrested back control of the island, and in 1814 Tobago was formally ceded to Britain in the Treaty of Paris. During the next twenty years, English overseers brought in ten thousand Africans to work on the sugar, cotton, and indigo plantations. It was a boom time for the production of all three. The abolition of slavery in 1834 brought about a change to free labor, but African freedmen also took to farming, and fishing communities sprang up around the island's coasts.

Collapse of the Sugar Trade

The lucrative sugar trade took a severe hit from a hurricane in 1847, and the industry was dealt another blow by the collapse of the West India Bank, which underwrote the sugar plantations. The decline of Tobago's sugar industry was further hastened by Britain's removal of protective import duties, thereby debasing the price paid for Tobago's sugar.

With the sugar industry on the slide, some of the land was turned into coconut, cocoa, and lime plantations but Tobago was plunged into economic ruin. And, in 1899, twenty years after Tobago had become a Crown Colony, the British effectively turned their back on the island. They had exploited its sugar trade to the hilt and, now that it was in serious recession, they retained scant interest in it. Broke and in debt, the island had little choice but to become a ward of Trinidad— but it was another twenty-eight years before Tobago was granted a seat on the Joint Legislative Council.

In 1963, Tobago suffered terrible damage from Hurricane Flora, which killed thirty, destroyed thousands of homes, and devastated crops. The recovery process was painful and slow and led to the gradual addition of tourism as a means of propping up the battered economy.

As joint islands, Trinidad and Tobago gained independence in 1962 and became a republic in 1976. Once Tobago's Crown Point Airport was upgraded to international status in 1985, with a lengthened runway and a new terminal building, the economy steadily benefited from an expansion in tourism. In 1998 Tobago was still officially rated

enough of an underdeveloped and low-income island to qualify for help from the UN and EC but recent years have seen a boom in tourism.

THE ECONOMY

Trinidad and Tobago is the leading producer of oil and natural gas in the Caribbean and the leading exporter of liquefied natural gas (LNG) to the United States. The country's economy is heavily dependent upon these resources. Oil and gas, accounting for about 40 percent of GDP and 80 percent of exports, generate huge revenues.

Investments in LNG, petrochemicals, and steel helped economic growth between 2000 and 2007 to average over 8 percent, more than double the

average for the region in that same period. It has since slowed down and in 2009 it contracted by around 2.7 percent, affected by the impact of the global economic downturn. Trinidad also felt the effects of lower energy prices, but a raft of new fiscal incentives planned by the government for the energy sector made for predictions of recovery in 2010 and an economic growth of 4 percent in 2011 and 5–6 percent in 2012.

Tobago's economy is tightly allied to Trinidad's, but tourism, and more recently ecotourism, is increasingly important.

GOVERNMENT
The Executive

The president of the republic is the head of state; Trinidad and Tobago follows the Westminster model of government and upholds the traditions of parliamentary democracy it inherited from Britain. The Parliament has a Senate and a House of Representatives. There are thirty-one members of the Senate, who are appointed by the president on the advice of the prime minister and the leader of the opposition. Legislative power lies with forty-one members in the House of Representatives elected by popular vote. A parliamentary term lasts five years unless a general election

is called **earlier**. Tobago has its own elected House of Assembly responsible for the administration of the island.

Former Attorney General Kamla Persad-Bissessar became Trinidad and Tobago's first woman prime minister in May 2010. She heads the United National Congress (UNC), which put together a coalition of five opposition parties, including Congress of the People (COP) and trade unions, to oust Patrick Manning's People's National Movement (PNM) in a general election. The political parties are very largely defined by race rather than ideals—the PNM is predominantly African, the UNC predominantly Indian, and the COP stands for multiracial socialism.

Manning had ruled the country for thirteen of the years since 1991 and his biggest accomplishments as prime minister included poverty reduction and attracting billions of

dollars in investment in Trinidad and Tobago's petrochemical industries. During his premiership he had come under criticism for mismanaging public funds, including spending on extravagant public buildings, and for corruption scandals. His defeat in a snap election was a political sea change because the PNM had ruled Trinidad and Tobago for most of the past fifty years.

The Judiciary

This arm of the state deals with enforcement of the criminal laws and the interpretation of the laws passed by Parliament (including the Constitution), as well as disputes between persons. Members of the Judiciary (the judges) are independent of the government and other authorities, and their appointment and terms of office are dealt with by an independent commission set up under the Constitution (the Judicial and Legal Service Commission). In this way they are insulated from any outside pressure and can make free, fair, and objective decisions. The judicial structure consists of a Supreme Court made up of the High Court, Magistrates' Courts, and other Tribunals. The Court of Appeal hears appeals from the High Court, Magistrates' Courts, and other Tribunals. In certain cases there is a right of appeal from the Court of Appeal to the Judicial Committee of Her Majesty's Privy Council (the Privy Council) in England.

chapter two

VALUES & ATTITUDES

Trinis are generally easygoing, happy, essentially religious, and well-educated people. They live life at a leisurely pace, are slow to anger, and quick to walk away from confrontation, though often they treat life's difficulties with resignation rather than action. Friendly, outgoing, and mostly devout, they have an infectious *joie de vivre* and a laid-back attitude to time. Life operates on "Trini time." Trinbagonians will tell you they can always spot a foreigner on a beach: he will be the one walking along the shore twice as fast as everyone else.

RELIGION

No fewer than fourteen national holidays reflect the Trinbagonian devotion to religion as well as their readiness to celebrate it joyously.

In this multiethnic society there is an admirable respect for other people's beliefs, which goes way beyond mere tolerance. It extends to an open, all-inclusive invitation and encouragement to join in religious celebrations, whatever one's faith. Typical of this is the Church of La Divina Pastora, which is a focus of devotion for Christians and non-Christians alike. On Holy Thursday and Good

Friday both Roman Catholics and Hindus visit the church to pay homage to La Divina Pastora and give thanks for the power of her intercession. Similarly, followers of all faiths are welcome to join in the celebrations of the Hindu festival of Diwali. This generosity of spirit

brings a harmonious cohesion to otherwise disparate communities, who tend to congregate in certain areas with others who share their beliefs.

THE FAMILY

Every celebration will be family-oriented because Trinis place great emphasis on the family unit, and a great deal of socializing is family-based. Trinidad and Tobago are both small islands and, unlike larger countries where families tend to disperse, the vast majority of a Trini's relatives are therefore within easy reach, unless they have gone abroad. Social gatherings will involve all family members, from great-grandmother down to the newborn baby. Children are included, cared for, and welcomed in T&T society, and not regarded as encumbrances.

THE LIME

Trinis are never happier than when they are
enjoying a "lime"—a leisurely gathering of good
friends and family for a chat and drinks, usually
rum, whether it be at the beach, by a river, or at
home. This national pastime has given rise to
the verb "to lime."

PRIDE AND PROMISES

One value all Trinis share is a sense of individual
self-worth. The history of the islands is record of
submission to foreign powers, and they dislike any
display of self-importance, any hint of superiority
or arrogance, from foreigners. Trinis expect to be
treated with respect and dignity, and they are
anxious not to appear inferior in any way.

In their eagerness to be helpful and on a par
with a foreigner, promises are made that may not
be easy to fulfill. The tendency is to say something
is achievable when what they actually mean is
they would like it to be. Tomorrow you may find
that their "yes" is not possible, and telephoning

you to tell you the bad news is not easy for them. Similarly, when asked a question, Trinis would rather hazard an answer than admit that they don't know. And when things don't work out as planned, their religious conviction can produce a shrug and the response that this is what fate decreed. This calm resignation is a way of dealing with setbacks.

ATTITUDES TOWARD FOREIGNERS

Because of the islands' ethnic diversity, Trinbagonians are tolerant of foreigners. Given the country's history, though, there is still a lingering suspicion that foreigners are there to take something away from them. Foreigners are regarded as transient, and Trinis are therefore reluctant to form deep friendships with them until they have lived in T&T for at least two years. In Trinidad, foreigners are regarded as visitors, whereas in Tobago, which is much more of a vacation isle, they are treated as tourists.

LACK OF NATIONAL IDENTITY

While there is personal and religious pride, national pride is much less evident. It was not so very long ago that everyone, relatively speaking, was an immigrant, and thus there is no definitive national identity, no sense of collective ownership of the land. This does not translate well in terms of Trinbagonians pulling together to care for and nurture their country, and to clean up their own backyard.

Tobago, which relies heavily on tourism for its economy, is much more aware of the way the world perceives it and is therefore cleaner, more eco-conscious, and more concerned with encouraging national pride.

ATTITUDES TOWARD THE LAW

Trinidad, in particular, has a huge crime problem and there is a general lack of respect for the law and for authority. This is possibly partly the legacy of slavery, when to defy or evade authority was an assertion of one's freedom. But it is also partly because today a lot of laws, such as those for driving offenses and building regulations, are not enforced. Lack of transparency has not helped either. In recent decades Trinis have seen too many instances of high-ranking government officials caught transgressing the law and escaping punishment. It has set a bad example.

SENSE OF HUMOR

Trinis laugh easily, especially at themselves. They see the funny side of life and often express this in calypsos, which can take the form of political satire, risqué jokes, or witty puns. The ability to make people laugh with jokes or tall stories is highly prized during limes. Interisland rivalry also means that regional jokes always go down well: Barbadian Bajans are humorously depicted as stupid, Jamaicans as violent, and Guyanese as dishonest. And when it comes to their own shortcomings, Trinis are no less pointed. Here's their take on the police.

Getting Results

A Trini man late one night spotted three men breaking into his garage and telephoned the police, only to be told there was no one available to attend the crime scene. A few minutes later he phoned the police again to say not to bother to come as he had shot dead all three robbers. Five minutes later an ambulance and four police cars arrived, and the police were amazed to find the robbers very much alive and captured them all. "I thought you said you'd shot them all dead," said the police chief. To which the man replied: "I thought you said no one was available."

LOVE OF MUSIC

Trinis are also famous for their love of music— the louder the better. Music is everywhere, in taxis, on the streets, in bars, at gatherings by the rivers, on the beaches, at the cricket grounds. Be prepared for loud music to accompany almost every kind of social occasion in Trinidad and Tobago. Some foreigners find the continuous Caribbean beat too noisy, insistent, and tiring. Requests to turn the volume down may be met with a reminder that music played loudly is part of the culture.

WORK ETHIC

Although in business many Trinis work long hours and share the ambitions of people in other capitalist countries, they place a greater emphasis on a stress-free life. Trinis generally work as a means to live, rather than the other way round. And it is generally accepted that the African community work to spend their money on enjoying themselves, whereas the Indian community keep their money and build on it.

GENDER

In what has been for generations a predominantly patriarchal society, there are issues around the changing role of men. However, while many women have reached high positions in business, particularly in marketing and PR, it is the men who still hold the purse strings.

Open displays of affection in public between members of the opposite sex are tolerated. Kissing in public and walking with arms around each other are not taboo provided there is no hint of lewd or blatantly physical behavior.

Homosexuality, on the other hand, is not tolerated by Christians or Muslims, on religious and social grounds. There is a homosexual community, but gays live a largely secret life, although they can be more open about their sexuality in artistic circles.

CLASS AND RACE

All Trinis have equal opportunities in education and health; they have the right to protest and freedom of speech in newspapers and on the radio and TV. Class issues are defined by wealth and education, and only to a very small extent ethnicity. Because so many of the population are of mixed race, racist attitudes are rare. Some wariness and suspicion does exist but it rarely leads to violent expression. Derogatory remarks or comments are generally restricted to light, humorous jibes in song.

MANNERS

Trinis are polite on the whole, but in an informal way. They may not stand upon ceremony, or open a door or pull out a chair for a woman, but they do like to be protective. They can also be surprisingly forthright. Comments on appearance, which foreigners might find rude, are not considered, or meant to be, disrespectful. A happy greeting followed by the observation that "you're puttin' on size" is not delivered as a barb but as a compliment, because slim is not necessarily considered to be the ideal figure. In this multiethnic society, manners and attitudes toward women differ widely and largely reflect the religious dictates, customs, and traditions of a person's background.

CUSTOMS & TRADITIONS

HOLIDAYS AND FESTIVALS

Barely a week goes by without some cause for mass celebration and every religious event is the signal for festivities. There are no fewer than fourteen national holidays, and many other days when, although they are not officially recognized, the country enjoys what is in effect a public holiday in all but name. The most famous of these is Carnival, which takes place over two days in February or March on the Monday and Tuesday before Ash Wednesday, the first day of Lent. (See page 72.) Carnival Monday and Tuesday are not official holidays, but nevertheless banks, schools, and shops are closed and most businesses shut down except those servicing Carnival.

Many religious festivals, especially Diwali, Hosay, and Christmas, are also attended and enjoyed by people other than the followers of the particular faith, and the numbers are swelled by a general unwritten invitation to all-comers to join in.

Hindu festivals are declared according to local astronomical observations and variations in dates may occur. Muslim festivals are timed according to local sightings of various phases of the moon and the dates given below are approximations. The actual dates are determined one to two weeks beforehand.

When a public holiday falls on a Sunday, it will be observed on the Monday that immediately follows. When two public holidays fall on the same date the following day is also a public holiday. The prime minister has the power to declare any date a public holiday.

NATIONAL HOLIDAYS
Christmas Day, Boxing Day, New Year's Day, Good Friday, and Easter Monday are all public holidays.

Christmas
Christmas is widely celebrated, with shopping malls displaying traditional decorations and Christmas trees. Trinis decorate their houses and even their cars during the Christmas period.

Traditional food served during the festivities includes ham, turkey, pastelles (corn parcels), sweet breads, and black cake, along with ginger beer (from the ginger root) and sorrel (a nonalcoholic drink brewed from the flowering bud of the sorrel tree), and punche de crème, a Caribbean eggnog made with citrus and rum. It's a season for large gatherings of family and friends, often swelled by visits by *paranderos*—groups similar to European and American carol singers who go from house to house serenading with indigenous Spanish carols know as parang (see page 107).

New Year's Eve

New Year's Eve is known as Old Year's Night and is the signal for typically Trini celebrations—large fetes comprising loud music by live bands, wild dancing, feasting, copious rum, and fireworks. The following are also national holidays.

Spiritual Baptist Shouters' Liberation Day (March 30)

This commemorates the abolition in 1951, after a long struggle, of the British-instituted Shouters' Prohibition Ordinance, which banned this religion in 1917 for effectively making too much noise. Developed among people of African descent during the nineteenth century, it combines elements of Protestant Christianity with African doctrines and rituals. Finally freed to practice their loud and demonstrative faith, the Spiritual Baptist Shouters were given further recognition by the state by being granted an annual public holiday.

Indian Arrival Day (May 30)

This day marks the arrival in Trinidad of the first indentured laborers from India in May 1845. Celebrated in Trinidad and Tobago for many years, it was only in 1994 that it was made an official public holiday, to commemorate the 140,000 Indians who were transported to the islands between 1845 and 1917. Most celebrations include the construction of replicas of the ship *Fatel Rozack*, which brought the first 225 Indian immigrants to Trinidad after 103 days at sea.

Corpus Christi

Dating back to Spanish times, the Catholic celebration of the Real Presence of Christ in the Eucharist is a public holiday. It occurs on the first Thursday following Trinity Sunday, which is usually the first Thursday before Easter. Observances take place in Port of Spain, San Fernando, Scarborough, and other parishes across the country. Roman Catholics attend church services on Corpus Christi morning and take part in processions in their communities. The largest is held in front of the Roman Catholic cathedral at Independence Square in Port of Spain.

Labor Day (June 19)

This is held annually on June 19, the anniversary of the workers' day of protest in 1937, which in essence led to the recognition of the modern trade union movement. Celebrations tend to be most public in Fyzabad in southern Trinidad, where the link with the Oil Workers' Union is particularly strong. Otherwise celebrations are minimal, and locals are more likely simply to enjoy having a day off.

Emancipation Day (August 1)

Trinidad was the first country in the world to declare a national public holiday to mark August 1,

1838, the day when slaves were granted full freedom. (Following the abolition of slavery in 1834 there was a four-year transition period in which ex-slaves were "apprenticed" to their former masters.) It's an important occasion given that many in Trinidad are descended from the thousands of slaves who worked and lived in desperately poor conditions on the sugar plantations. Finally accorded their freedom, they set up new villages such as Belmont, Arouca, and Laventille.

In the days leading up to Emancipation Day, it is a common sight to see people dressed in traditional African clothes in proud reaffirmation of their heritage. Celebrations include Kambule, a colorful, rhythmic procession through the streets of Port of Spain, and the Flambeaux procession in which participants walk with lighted torches.

Tobago celebrates Emancipation Day with the Great Race, a speedboat race from Trinidad to Tobago. Chaguaramas is the morning starting point for the race and the celebrations gather steam in the afternoon at the finishing line at Tobago's Store Bay.

Independence Day (August 31)
This marks the day, August 31, 1962, when the Union Jack, the British national flag, was finally lowered and Trinidad and Tobago became an

independent nation. It is now a part of the British
Commonwealth. Celebrations include a daytime
parade by members of the Trinidad and Tobago
Defense Force in Queen's Park, inspected by the
head of state in Trinidad and the chief secretary in
Tobago. National awards for various achievements
follow in the evening at the president's house and
culminate in firework displays.

Eid-ul-Fitr (date varies)

Often abbreviated to Eid, this festival marks the
end of Ramadan, the Muslim month of ritual
fasting. On the first day, a Muslim family gets up
at sunrise to attend special prayers in mosques held
only for the occasion. After prayers there are visits
to the homes of friends and family and a common
greeting is "*Eid Mubarak*," which means "Happy
Eid" or "Blessed Eid." For Muslims, Eid is a time to
come together as a community and to help the
needy. Because the Muslim lunar calendar is eleven
days shorter than the solar year, the festival moves
in relation to the Gregorian calendar. The actual

dates for Eid are announced one to two weeks prior to their observance each year.

Republic Day (September 24)
Although Trinidad and Tobago became a republic on August 1, 1976, the event is celebrated on September 24, which marks the date when the first Parliament met under the new republican constitution.

Diwali (date varies)
Since 43 percent of the population are ethnic Indians, the Hindu festival of Diwali (otherwise known as the Festival of Lights) is an important celebration. The observation of this festival by Trinidad's Indian communities is one of the largest outside India. It is marked by dozens of events filled with jubilation, togetherness, and pageantry, as well as the usual religious rituals. Government ministers sometimes participate in the festivities, which continue for over a week.

The focal point is the HQ of the National Council of Indian Culture at Divali Nagar in the town of Chaguanas. Although Diwali is a Hindu festival, it is a national holiday observed by all religious denominations. It is celebrated with prayers and feasts, and climaxes in the lighting of thousands of *deyas* all over the country. These are small earthen lamps made from clay pots filled with oil in which a wick is immersed. The lamps are lit to symbolize the triumph of light over darkness, knowledge over ignorance, and in honor of Lakshmi, the goddess of light, beauty, riches, and love. The pots are often attached to bamboo stalks bent into imaginative shapes and designs, thereby illuminating entire villages and communities. Diwali is one of the most anticipated events in Trinidad and, in the weeks leading up to the festival, stories of the origin of Diwali are acted out in full costume in open-air theaters and villages. The actual date of Diwali is announced one to two weeks before the observance each year.

OTHER RELIGIOUS FESTIVALS

Phagwa, or Holi (date varies)

This is a spring festival that takes place on the
first day of the full moon in the month of Phagun
(February to early March) to celebrate the Hindu
New Year. It was introduced to Trinidad by
indentured East Indian laborers around 1845.
It has religious significance as a rite of
purification to promote good health. The festival
includes singing and dancing, with mock battles
where neighbors, friends, and other participants
spray each other with *abeer* (magenta watercolor
dyes), using large syringelike instruments called
pichkarees, and exchange sweets. The festival is
regarded as the time for learning, bonding,
communal sharing, and togetherness.

Hosay (between May and June, according to the Islamic lunar calendar)

The Islamic festival of Hosay, known elsewhere as
Yaum Ashura, was first held in Trinidad in 1854
and commemorates the martyrdom of Hussain,
the grandson of the Prophet Muhammad, in the
year 680 CE. There is prayer and fasting, and Hosay

parades take place in two
Shiite communities in
Trinidad: St. James, in the
western section of Port of
Spain, and Cedros, in the
south. The colorful
procession in St. James
is the largest and draws
thousands of spectators of

all religions. The Shiites of St. James spend a considerable amount of time and money in the building of miniature temples and mausoleums (known as *tadjahs, taziyas,* or *hosays*) with bamboo, wood, paper, and tinsel to depict the tomb of Hussain. These *tadjahs* range in height from 10 to 30 feet (3 to 9 m) and are hauled through the streets on parade days accompanied by the beating of drums *(tassas)* and two standards in the shape of half-moons, each carried on the shoulders of bearers. The half-moons, one for Hussain and the other for his brother Hassan, are significant parts of the procession.

FURTHER CELEBRATIONS
Feast of La Divina Pastora (May)
The church of La Divina Pastora at Siparia is unusual in that it is a focus of prayer for Christians and non-Christians alike. On Holy Thursday and Good Friday Hindus and Roman Catholics visit the church to pay homage to La Divina Pastora and give thanks for the power of her intercession. Because of the unique nature of the devotions that take place at La Divina Pastora the church has been, and continues to be, the subject of research by undergraduate and graduate students of the University of the West Indies, as well as foreign universities.

Pan Ramajay (May)

A monthlong festival of steel band music across
T&T, with small-pan ensembles playing a wide
selection of music, which ranges from jazz to
classical.

St. Peter's Day (June 29 or nearest weekend)

T&T's fishing communities celebrate with major
fetes on the beaches, fueled by fish broth and loud
sound systems.

Santa Rosa Festival (August)

This is an annual festival held in Arima in north
central Trinidad to honor the patron saint of the
local Caribbean Amerindian community.
Celebrations include services in the saint's praise
and the carrying aloft of her statue through the
streets before she is returned to her rightful place
in the Santa Rosa church. A parade and dancing
to parang music form part of the celebrations.

Ramleela (September or October)

This is a special event where communities come
together for nine days to reenact stories from
the Hindu epic the *Ramayana*. Excerpts are read
and performed by dancers in brightly colored
costumes and at the end an effigy of the villain
Ravana is burned, symbolizing the triumph of
good over evil.

Chinese Arrival Day (October 12)

This is an annual celebration to mark the arrival
in Trinidad in 1806, on the ship *Fortitude*, of 192

Chinese men, the first organized settlement of
Chinese in the Americas. The day is celebrated
with indigenous dishes, music, dance, and art,
and dragon boat races.

Ramadan
The Muslim community observes the holy
month of Ramadan, the ninth lunar month of
the Islamic year, with fasting from dawn until
sunset. The fast, which is one of the Five Pillars
of Islam, is the primary form of the observance.
Ramadan is a time when Muslims are
encouraged to perform extra acts of worship
and charity.

Trinidad & Tobago Awards (October)
This is the islands' equivalent of the Grammys,
in which prizes are handed out to the cream of
musicians in all areas of T&T's music scene.

World Steel Band Festival (October)
Concerts are staged around Trinidad showcasing
the top steel bands playing a specially composed
piece for the competition as well as current
calypso and classical music, and other popular
tunes.

National Folk Festival (October–November)
This is a nationwide event in which villages
provide competitors for various Port of Spain
contests including dance, music, acting, and
cooking, with the prime minister announcing
the winner.

Pan Jazz Festival (November)

Financial constraints have made this less than an annual festival, but when staged it showcases pan ensembles from all over the world. Tickets aren't cheap but there is usually a chance to catch a free night's entertainment at Brian Lara Promenade in Port of Spain.

SPECIAL EVENTS ON TOBAGO

In addition to the earlier general holidays, Tobago stages a major festival or event every few months and mini-festivals every month.

Goat and Crab Races (Easter weekend)

Big open-air parties and feasts are the preliminaries to Easter Tuesday's Buccoo goat races, which are taken seriously enough to warrant a fenced-in track, starting gates, a scoreboard, jockeys, and races sponsored by local businesses. The crab races are taken less seriously but the moment they are over is the signal for wild, all-night partying, music, and dancing.

Tobago Jazz Festival (April)

This festival at Plymouth attracts international headliners and past superstar performers include Sir Elton John, Rod Stewart, and Sting. Like many of the region's jazz festivals, there is more rock 'n roll, rhythm and blues, soca, and reggae than pure jazz. Usually held over three days, the festival attracts around 40,000 patrons. Some shows are free.

Charlotteville Fisherman's Fete (July)

One of Tobago's biggest fetes celebrates the income and sustenance generated for the islanders by fishing. It's usually a noisy, vibrant all-night beach party.

Tobago Heritage Festival (July–August)

Spanning a two-week period, the festival is Tobago's cultural showpiece and is held all over the island to celebrate Tobago's traditions of dance, music, storytelling, culture, and cuisine. It has a new theme every year, with each village staging a signature event. It starts and finishes with a gala opening and parades in Scarborough and some of the major events include speech bands (which give voice to issues of political and social importance, often with a humorous or satirical twist), folk reenactment, sports events, and an old-time Tobago wedding ceremony, which usually takes place in Moriah.

The wedding ceremony is a signature Tobago Heritage Festival event where islanders, some as young as nine, dress up in classic wedding gear

and parade through the streets. The event is not just an entertainment. Some of the rituals promote fertility and the ceremony is used as a way of passing on communal customs, traditions, and values such as purity and fidelity.

There is a Sea Festival in Black Rock, a Ms Heritage Personality competition in Scarborough, and Wake and Bongo in Charlotteville, which evokes the mystical side of Tobagonian culture, filled with rituals that combine Christian and African religious elements. The wake is a night ceremony to honor the dead with Christian hymns and feasting, an African-devised custom. The bongo is characterized by suggestive dancing and risqué songs designed to encourage merriment and sexual arousal with the aim of exhorting the participants to make love and thereby create new life.

Great Fete and Carib Great Race (August)
First staged in 1969, the 84-mile speedboat race from the Gulf of Paria in Trinidad to Crown Point in Tobago ends in the ultimate five-day beach party at Store Bay, Pigeon Point, and Mount Irvine.

Tobago Fest (October 3 to 5)
This is a carnival-themed festival including a parade of bands, art, exhibitions, and fetes. It opens with a Festival Queen competition in Roxborough, followed next morning by a J'ouvert parade in Plymouth. (J'ouvert is an opening day event, from the French *ouvrir* meaning to open.) Later, Scarborough hosts a parade of costumed bands on its streets. The following day there is a beach fete at Store Bay.

chapter four

MAKING
FRIENDS

Trinbagonians are warm and friendly by nature
and it is easy to make acquaintances, but it may
take a while for a foreigner to form a firm
friendship. However, Trinis are hospitable and
keen to look after visitors, to tell them the best
places to go, to impart their local knowledge,
and to help them make the most of their visit.

For Trinbagonians, a true friend is someone
who is loyally supportive through thick and thin,
and who is likely to practice the same religion.
Close friendships are often forged at school or
later at work, fully blossom between adults, and
are expected to last through life. In such small
islands, good friends meet very regularly.

Foreigners can find it extremely difficult to
break into a circle of Trini friends. This is largely

because they are regarded as being just visitors, nothing more. They are seen as passing through. It takes two years of at least semipermanent residency before a foreigner will be considered worthy of something stronger than a mere acquaintanceship.

You are unlikely to be invited into the home of a business contact until a firm and lasting friendship has been forged. A foreigner is much more likely to be taken out to lunch by a contact, and spouses rarely attend such lunches or dinners unless it is a particular function, such as a Christmas dinner, where a wife or partner is specifically included.

FRIENDS WITH FOREIGNERS

We've seen that foreigners in Trinidad are treated differently from foreigners in Tobago. In Trinidad they are regarded as visitors, in Tobago as tourists—and the difference is marked.

Trinidadians regard foreigners as equals whereas Tobagonians tend to be more respectful and polite because they know their island's economy relies to a large extent on tourism and they want and need you to come back. They are not servile, but the attitude in Trinidad is more genuine. While Trinidadians are respectful of visitors to their shores they are not subservient or overly polite. They simply show a healthy interest and no resentment whatsoever of your being there if they meet you. And, if they don't make your acquaintance, they allow you to go about your business without hassle.

It's only when there's an international cricket match taking place in Port of Spain that foreigners tend to be seen in Trinidad in very large groups, as each cricket-playing country now has a substantial army of traveling fans. With a common love for the game, there is friendly rivalry, no little banter, and rarely any trouble when fans cram into the bars. Given the islands' history of being fought over and ruled by foreigners for centuries, any sort of patronizing behavior should be avoided, and an appreciation of the culture of the twin islands is essential.

MEETING PEOPLE
Bars and Nightclubs

There is barely a corner of Trinidad without at least a basic roadside bar where you can sing karaoke and perhaps shoot pool while slaking your thirst. In towns all over Trinidad and Tobago there are traditional rum shops, very basic bars that may be little more than glorified shacks serving alcohol. There is at least one in every village, possibly selling a few other provisions as well.

Most bars on both islands are not too bothered about décor, but, beyond the basics, there are upscale bars and fashionable lounges with chic interiors in Port of Spain and in Crown Point in Tobago, some featuring large screen TVs showing popular sports matches. After work on a Friday is a favorite time to go to a bar and drinking hours are not restricted.

Trinidad, but not Tobago, has a limited club scene thanks to the opening of one or two elegant nightspots in Port of Spain. The Trini love of a party has fueled the emergence of mega-clubs with several levels and special VIP areas. The more exclusive clubs require ID to get in and operate invitation lists and a strict dress code.

Although most hotels in Tobago provide entertainment nightly, nobody goes to this island for the nightlife. The hotels regularly feature bands playing typically Trinbagonian music to dance to and there are some restaurants with areas in which to dance. But outside the Crown Point area of Tobago and in rural localities, nightlife consists of nothing more than a bar or two in which to meet the locals and it is rare to find one still open at 11:00 p.m.

Fetes, usually held in the open air, are the focal points for nightlife on both islands. "All-inclusive fetes" are the most popular. A ticket entitles you to dance into the small hours to a selection of bands and to eat and drink as much as you like. Trinidad's biggest fetes around Carnival time attract a gathering of many hundreds of people all out to have a good time, with tickets costing as much as $TT500 (about US$80, or £50) for the very best ones.

The ideal way for resident foreigners to make friends is through sports activities, joining special interest clubs or associations, reading groups, hiking clubs, and attending church-related functions. It's a cultural trait among Trinis to share and that extends to putting foreigners in touch with friends, family, or acquaintances who have similar interests.

Socializing
Historians claim that the Africans and Indians who first arrived in Trinidad came from areas in their

respective countries that were known for their celebrations. So it is probably no coincidence that Trinis like to go out and have a good time. Most socializing in rural areas is conducted in the rum shops. But throughout Trinidad and Tobago families frequently visit each other and their respective children get to know each other from their early years.

In this diverse society people happily mix with other races and classes, and it is only the Syrians who tend to lead very insular lives. You just have to attend a large fete to realize how mixed the races are. People from all echelons of society and from all religions, creeds, and cultures gather and mingle harmoniously.

Some of the stricter, older traditions among the Indian population have eased. The academically motivated Indian youth have been well educated for many years now, and they are more aspirational, worldly, and socially aware than previous generations. Hence they are more independent, more individual, and less tied to their families or bound by their customs.

Trinidad and Tobago is a reasonably egalitarian society though, as we have seen, there is some elitism due to the oldest Trini families being white. Such divisions as do exist are defined by religion, racial heritage, or education. Trinis have an expression— "no brought-upsie"—for the uneducated and those who don't know how to behave.

Among the poorer sections of the population, families integrate more with each other because they are more often in each other's yards, whereas the trend for high-rise living among the better off is isolating.

GREETINGS

Trinis don't stand on ceremony. As long as you are open and friendly, you will be assured of a warm greeting. A handshake is considered polite, but make it a firm one as a weak handshake is considered insincere. Don't be confused if someone says "Hello, goodnight." They are not saying goodbye—it is the Trini way of saying good evening. Locals tend to speak of 3:00 p.m. or 4:00 p.m. as the evening.

While handshakes are the normal greeting, the African version of gentle knuckle punching, high fives, and exchange of handclaps are common among firm friends.

INVITATIONS HOME

It's an honor to be invited to a Trinbagonian's home for lunch or dinner, and it is polite to accept. Such an invitation is common once a friendship has been established. Traditionally the host is expected to provide everything but it is not an inappropriate gesture to ask if there is anything you can bring to add to the meal. Taking a bottle of wine is not mandatory but it will be welcomed if you do, especially if you have asked your hosts beforehand what wine they prefer. Taking a bottle of rum or beer is not the done thing, unless it is a beach party or a casual lime; wine is an acceptable offering for a dinner because it will have been imported and is therefore special. Trinis are not big on receiving flowers or a plant, except at Christmas, when a poinsettia is a seasonal gift.

Guests rarely arrive on time, not just because they have been delayed in traffic but because flexibility when it comes to time is a way of life. Anything up to forty minutes is acceptably late. If it is a sit-down lunch or dinner, a Trini host will wait until all the guests have arrived before starting the meal. But this general rule does not apply if it is simply a lime with drinks and help-yourself food.

If it is a family occasion, it is polite to offer to help with preparing the food, but not if the meal is with a business contact. Many will use catering companies anyway. Trinis enjoy providing a real spread with the emphasis on the main course and a dessert; it will be considered impolite if you leave immediately after the meal. You will be expected to socialize for some while after you have dined and, rather than coffee signaling the conclusion of the meal, the norm is to carry on drinking. At the end of the evening, the polite host will walk you either to the door or to your car.

SOCIALIZING WITH THE OPPOSITE SEX

Despite their laid-back reputation and evident enjoyment of life, Trinis are basically conservative and mindful of their reputations. Socializing with the opposite sex is not easy for foreigners. Regarded simply as visitors, their transience marks them down as unsuitable as meaningful partners. The African community is less rigid about forming relationships with foreigners than the Indian community, for whom traditional religious mores and customs tend to hold sway.

Trinidad and Tobago are small islands where gossip is rife and travels fast, and women in particular are extremely careful about how they are seen, often keeping their private lives separate from their social lives.

chapter five

PRIVATE & FAMILY LIFE

THE FAMILY

The family is central to Trinbagonian society, particularly in Indian communities. It is common for parents to see their children every day, even when they are grown up and have left home. Relatives tend to live nearby, older ones are cared for, and it is a rare weekend when they are not all gathered together from great-grandmother downward. While the previous generation was more patriarchal, among younger Trinis there is greater equality between the sexes. On the downside, the changing role of the male has created social problems, which sometimes result in domestic violence.

DAILY LIFE

In the Town

Most people in Trinidad and Tobago live in towns in busy, overcrowded, congested areas with rapidly expanding programs of residential development. In Trinidad, building continues apace, with the Housing Development Corporation on an aggressive drive to build

100,000 housing units at an estimated 10,000 units a year. A lot of old houses are being torn down to make way for apartment complexes, gated communities, and town house complexes. The kind of home in which people live varies according to cultural background and income.

Families rise early, often at 5:30 a.m., and go to bed early during the week, usually around 10:00 p.m. Breakfast, which is not necessarily eaten together, is likely to consist of fruit, eggs, bacon, and creole bake. A proper lunch is an important meal for Trinis and workplaces cater to this accordingly. Because lunch is the main meal

of the day, there is no sandwich culture in T&T. Those who work within easy reach of their homes will go home for lunch. Popular lunch fare includes doubles or rotis (see pages 84–5). Middle-income people generally commute to work by car for anything up to an hour and a half.

It is the woman of the house who does the shopping, usually at markets selling local produce, which open as early as 6:00 a.m. Most people shop at markets and stores, but Trinis on higher incomes tend to drive to supermarkets, which have a wider range of food and provisions.

Although Trinis are up for a party any night of the week, they look forward to socializing on weekends, which start at 5:00 p.m. on a Friday, usually with a drink. The middle and upper classes have maids to clean their houses, and a network of plumbers, electricians, mechanics, carpenters, and gardeners they can call on for help with anything from air-conditioning problems to termites. The better, more reliable workmen and firms are highly prized by foreigners, who can be driven to distraction by workers who continually arrive late or not at all.

In the Country
Rural life is much slower, quieter, and simpler than in the towns. Ambitions in the rural areas are also much lower than in the towns, and life is basically a success if there is enough food on the table for the family and a roof over their heads. In the poorer sections of society, particularly among African Trinis, the lack of a sense of responsibility

toward wife and family on the part of the menfolk is a problem. Thus there are many single-parent families and a lot of children are brought up by just their mothers and/or their

grandparents. Many mothers work because the father is absent or not working—and is not compelled to do so.

In Tobago, the pace of life is gentler still. A sleepy atmosphere pervades many of the little villages and smaller coastal fishing communities.

GROWING UP IN TRINIDAD AND TOBAGO

Children are brought up according to the tenets of their respective religions. But, while the

Catholic community adheres to its principles and, for example, strictly forbids couples to live together before marriage, the Indian community is facing challenges to its own traditional mores and customs. The influence of nearby America and multichannel American TV has given the young an enlarged view of life outside T&T. As a result they are far more worldly than their parents and are keen to live their own lives free of certain traditions. Educated Indian girls in particular are growing up wanting more of a say in their own lives, particularly when it comes to whom they will marry.

The majority of children live at home with their families until they get married or move abroad to study or to work. Most Trini teenagers are fully engaged with society, but boys growing up in poor areas face the danger of being lured into gangs with promises of smart clothes, cell phones, and other gadgets. Once a member of a gang, their leaders make it nigh on impossible for them to leave and return to the straight and narrow.

EDUCATION

There is a strong culture of education and learning in Trinbagonian society. The education system is similar to Britain's, with children generally starting preschool at the age of three before going on to primary school at five and secondary school at twelve. Primary and secondary education are free to everyone. There

also are fee-paying religious institutions and private schools, which are favored by the middle and upper classes. All schoolchildren wear uniforms. School is compulsory up to the age of sixteen and Trinbagonians are among the most basically well-educated people in the world, with a literacy rate of around 97 percent. In September 2004, Trinidad and Tobago joined other Caribbean islands in replacing the Cambridge University Examination Board's Advanced Levels with the Caribbean Advanced Proficiency Examinations (CAPE).

Families, particularly the Indian section of the population, encourage their children to do well at school, believing that a good education will be of benefit in the likely event they will at some stage move abroad for a better life.

Higher education is also free for all up to bachelor's degree level at the University of Trinidad and Tobago (UTT), the University of the West Indies (UWI), and the University of the

Southern Caribbean (USC). To attain developed nation status by 2020, the government has set a target of 60 percent college participation for the sixteen to twenty-five age group by 2015.

T&T has suffered from a "brain drain" and UTT was established by the government in 2004 with the specific aim of creating a skilled workforce closely fitted to the industrial and economic developmental needs of the country. This university offers many vocational and technical courses, often in oil and gas-related subjects, and is starting to slow the exodus. A campus of UWI offers courses in engineering, business administration, law, medicine, agriculture, humanities, and other subjects. USC is a private Seventh-day Adventist degree-granting institution.

CARNIVAL

It's impossible to overstate how much Carnival means to the people of Trinidad and Tobago. Officially it is two February days and nights of mass street celebration of music, exquisite costumes, and dance spread over the Monday and Tuesday before Lent. In reality Carnival casts its joyful exuberance over both islands, but especially Trinidad, all the year round. It's an ever-present industry showcasing many of the nation's most distinctive art forms. The moment Carnival ends, the islanders start planning for the next.

Carnival draws thousands of visitors to Port of Spain each year to watch and, better still, take part in the gaiety of what many believe to be the most spectacular show on earth. Trinidad's Carnival dates back to the 1780s, when French Catholic planters arrived on the islands and staged elaborate masquerade balls at Christmas and a "farewell to the flesh" before the Catholic Lenten season. Their African slaves had their own traditions of masquerade and held celebrations around the harvesting and burning of the sugar cane—known as *cannes brulees*, which came to be anglicized as Canboulay—at Carnival time.

Following the final emancipation of the slaves in 1838 Canboulay became an annual symbol of freedom. Then, in 1881, Carnival was engulfed in a violent crisis after an overbearing new English chief of police called Captain Baker was appointed to succeed a man noted for his "masterly inactivity." Baker took it upon himself to head a posse to put an end to Canboulay, believing that the torches the people carried were dangerous and that the stick fighting of the farm laborers was a threat to law and order.

Baker's attempt to clamp down upon the more subversive aspects of Carnival was construed by the people as a bid to destroy Carnival itself. His actions led to a riot and a bloody battle ensued between police and masqueraders. Ultimately the result was a suggestion by the governor of the day, Sir Sanford Freeling, that the people and the authorities should get together to agree on what form Carnival should take in the future. This evolved into the establishment of the schedule of events that have come to define Trinidadian identity.

CARNIVAL TIME

FRIDAY
"Fantastic Friday" sees stick fighters, moko jumbies— Trinis walking as ghosts on towering stilts up to 16 feet (5 meters) high—

and actors and dancers reenacting the Canboulay riots. In the early afternoon, traditional Carnival characters take the spotlight and soca stars battle for the Soca Monarch crowns in the evening.

SATURDAY
On the pre-Carnival Saturday, Port of Spain's streets and its central park, the Savannah, play host to Kiddies' Carnival, followed in the evening by Panorama, the finals of the steel band competitions. The authorities

have demolished the grandstand, and the temporary stand erected every year on the Savannah doesn't accommodate enough spectators. If you can't get a seat, the best way to hear the bands is to catch them practicing nearby before they take to the stage.

SUNDAY

Known as Dimanche Gras, this comprises
the Calypso Monarch competition, ole-time
Carnival, and the crowning of the King and
Queen of Carnival.

MONDAY

This is the official start of Carnival, known as
J'ouvert. Before dawn, thousands of people
swarm into the streets and "chip" (slow march
in time to the beat) and cavort through Port
of Spain and Trinidad's other towns and
cities, covered in paint, grease, mud or oil,

alongside traditional Carnival characters such
as blue devils, bats, and Jab Jabs—traditional
masque characters resembling impish devils.
Once the sun is up, revelers go off to breakfast
and rest, ready to return and resume the
celebrations around noon by following the
bands mounted on trucks with music
booming out at high decibels.

TUESDAY
Masqueraders are up early to follow their
bands as they parade through the streets past
various judging points where assessors work
out who should win the Band of the Year and
Road March titles. Some bands attract as
many as five thousand followers, many of
whom manage to dance right through the day
into the evening and beyond midnight (the
official end of Carnival) to what is known as
Last Lap, before arriving home in the early
hours.

WEDNESDAY
Ash Wednesday is not a holiday, but that
doesn't prevent Trinis from flocking to the
beaches to cool down and recover from two
days of unrivaled revelry.

Playing Mas

Some Carnival mas (masquerade) bands are launched as early as July, seven months before the actual event. This is when anyone can call in at the band's mas camp to view, and perhaps order, the costumes specially designed for the upcoming Carnival. Those who ally themselves to a band are known as "playing mas" and the costumes, many of which are incredibly extravagant and elaborate, may cost anything up to US$200 (£300). Some bands sell out from as early as September, but returns can be bought at the last minute.

After Christmas the buildup gathers steam, with parties held all over Trinidad catering to all tastes. Carnival fetes feature the biggest soca stars and the latest soca and pan tunes dominate the radio and TV airwaves, while masqueraders build up their stamina for what is known as the "wining season"—"wining" defines the high energy, often sexually overt, liquid-limbed style of dancing. Early January also sees the opening of calypso tents, and competitions begin for steel bands, soca singers, calypsonians, limbo dancers, stick fighters, costume designers, traditional Carnival characters, and Carnival Kings and Queens. Everywhere steel bands are to be found practicing in their panyards.

The week before Carnival is brim full of fetes, events, and competitions and the celebrations start to take on a formal schedule.

The combination of frenetic music rhythms pumping out from the trucks, the colorful costumes made with remarkable creativity and ingenuity, and the shared feeling of celebration all make for a stunning spectacle. Traditionalists resent the fact that so many of the female revelers go for bikini mas with skimpy costumes, feathers, and beads, which make them look like Las Vegas showgirls. But the work that goes into the more ambitious costumes, such as vast butterfly creations, is extraordinary and breathtaking by any standards.

Foreign spectators are advised not to look like tourists. Don't take anything valuable with you and stick to the main judging areas for your own safety. In past years the police have locked up potential troublemakers before Carnival started, but this is not always the case and foreigners have been robbed or hassled and had cameras stolen while distracted by the spectacle. It pays to be vigilant and, if playing mas and following a band, make yourself known to the band's substantial security teams. There are drink and food vendors all along the parade routes to keep you fortified for what can be an exhausting but exhilarating couple of days. Some bands pump out their music so loudly that they hand out earplugs. But if you are allergic to a booming bass, it's wise to take your own.

Every Trini insists that you cannot fully capture the spirit of Carnival unless you take an active part. The extraordinary state of elation that the revelers work themselves into is akin to the childlike joy of simply living in the moment, and deliriously sharing that euphoria with thousands of others who are feeling exactly the same way. No one has described it better than Nobel Prize-winner Derek Walcott: "It is exultation of the mass will, its hedonism is so sacred that to withdraw from it, not to jump up, to be a contemplative outside of its frenzy, is a heresy."

chapter six

TIME OUT

On Trinidad and Tobago's many national holidays and other festivals, beach or river limes are always popular. Families or groups of friends head for a day out together armed with plenty of food and drink and portable music. Sporting activities fill much of Trini leisure time and in the evening there are always fetes to attend, with music provided by a succession of live bands. Sports clubs and associations welcome visitors who display a genuine enthusiasm, and fetes are open to all for the price of a ticket.

TRINBAGONIAN CUISINE

Trinidad and Tobago's cuisine is as varied as its people, with each group of immigrants adding their own styles of food, ingredients, and recipes to those of the original Amerindians. It's therefore no surprise to find that the Spanish, French, English, Syrian/ Arabic, East Indian, and Chinese have brought their respective influences to bear upon Creole food, which is Trinidad and Tobago's very own.

Trinis love their food. If you are invited to a Trini home you will be offered something to eat and it would be impolite to refuse. Because the best dishes take a great deal of preparation and are difficult to make, home-cooked food is often tastier than in restaurants.

Fruits and Vegetables

T&T has a vast range of fruits that are eaten in season. Imported fruit is too expensive for much of the population, but many grocers and the big supermarket chain Hi Lo sell imported fruit and vegetables such as apples, pears and grapes, carrots, potatoes, and onions. Locally grown fruit includes banana, pawpaw, mango, pineapple,

grapefruit, lime, orange, pomerac, zaboca, sapodilla, tamarind, soursop, guava, and portugal—a popular, very sweet fruit like a clementine. Breadfruit, introduced to the islands by the British as cheap food for their slaves, can be fried, roasted, or boiled and served in soups. Plantain, rather like a large banana, is a fruit but is used as a vegetable to be boiled or fried or sliced thinly into chips.

The choice of fruit and vegetables in Tobago is more limited than in Trinidad, but vegetables, especially root vegetables such as yams, eddoes, tania, sweet potatoes, and cassava, are plentiful. Lettuce, cucumber, tomatoes, watercress, and chives are commonly available, but carrots and onions are imported. Food and other supplies in Tobago are best bought from grocery stores from Crown Point to Scarborough; the largest is in the neighborhood of Canaan. Cambee Scarborough market is best visited on a Friday or Saturday for vegetables, fruit, fish, and local foods.

Rice, which is both homegrown and imported, is an essential part of the national diet.

Meat
For the great majority of the population, chicken is easily available and cheap as it is subsidized. Some lamb and beef is imported. Little roast pork is eaten but bacon and baked ham is common, and curry goat is a popular dish. Most people in town buy meat from supermarkets, but in rural areas it's common for families either to keep chickens or goats or know people with a fowl who can kill it for you. Wild game meat, including agouti (a small species of rodent that looks like a guinea pig), quenk (a wild hog), and iguana, is rare but a staple of Tobago's harvest festivals.

Fish and Seafood
Fish is plentiful and eaten everywhere on both islands. Varieties range from shark, carite, dolphin, crayfish, king fish, flying fish, and red

snapper. Trinis will urge you to try cascadou because, according to legend, anyone who eats this fish will return to Trinidad. Those who keep

coming back to Trinidad are often greeted with the words: "You must have eaten cascadoux."

Oysters, which grow on the roots of the mangrove swamps outside Port of Spain, are popular and are offered by the plateful at busy intersections and at stalls around Trinidad's Savannah—Port of Spain's largest open space, consisting of 260 acres (105 ha) of flat grassland. Shrimp is bought frozen but uncooked, and, rarely seen in shops. What is considered a delicacy is Chip Chip— small shellfish found along the shores of Trinidad. For freshness it's best to collect these yourself on the beach, but it's a laborious process before you get to eat them. First you have to use your hands to scoop the tiny clams out of the sand where they live, and then thoroughly wash and strain them to get rid of the sand before extracting the meat— not easy since each shell contains less than a gram of meat. Trinis believe it is worth the effort.

Desserts

Trinis aren't big dessert eaters, but fruit and coconut desserts are popular, and they eat a lot of ice cream. Most of the well-known ice cream brand-names are available in a range of flavors at supermarkets and there are a variety of ice cream parlors in towns. Black cake, fruit cake soaked in rum, is commonly eaten at Christmas.

Some Local Specialties
Roti
The roti is an East Indian dish popular in both islands. It consists of an outer casing of thinly rolled cooked dough wrapped around highly

seasoned meat cooked with curry. Flavors can be chicken, goat, shrimp, beef, liver, or plain potato. Common vegetable fillings are channa (curried chickpeas), bodi (green beans), aloo (curried potato), pumpkin, or bhaji (special vegetable stir-fry). A variation of roti called paratha commonly sold as "buss up shut" ("buss up" meaning to eat hungrily) is shredded and used to scoop up the vegetables by hand. Aloo (or allou) pie or potato pie, a soft bake stuffed with potato and channa, is also very popular alongside roti.

Buljol (or Bull Johl)
A favorite Sunday morning breakfast dish, this is a mixture of desalted shredded codfish, chipped onions, tomatoes, dried avocado pear, sweet potatoes, black pepper, and olive oil. It's

best eaten with zaboca (avocado) and bake (sweet unleavened bread).

Doubles

Probably the most popular fast food in Trinidad and Tobago, doubles is basically a sandwich made with two flat fried breads and filled with curried chick peas, dhal (lentils), and channa (yellowish-brown peas) topped off with a variety of spicy chutneys such as mango, tamarind, coconut, and cucumber and pepper sauce. It's a common stomach-filling street food and popularly eaten for breakfast or as a late-night snack.

Calaloo

One of Trinidad's best-known dishes, this is a soup made from dasheen leaves with okra, coconut milk, green pepper, and lots of different flavorings, and boiled to the consistency of a thick soup. Calaloo is sometimes made with crab and often served with macaroni pie, stewed chicken, plantain, and rice and peas. For many Trinis, this is the perfect Sunday lunch.

Shark and Bake

This is T&T's version of fish and chips and no beach lime is complete without it. Cooked with lime juice, minced garlic, minced chives, and fresh thyme, shark and bake (the sweet, unleavened bread) is a specialty served at the roadside and at beachside stands at Maracas Bay, one of Trinidad's most popular beaches. Shark and "hops," a light, crusty bun, is a popular variation.

Pastelle
Seasoned meat, lentils, or soya, with olives, capers, and raisins in a cornmeal casing and steamed in banana leaves.

Souse
Pork boiled and served cold in a salty sauce with lime, cucumber, pepper, and onion slices.

Pelau
One-pot dish of rice and pigeon peas with meat.

DRINKS
Alcohol
Trinidad and Tobago has a strong drinking culture, partly due to local beers and rums being relatively inexpensive. Locally produced Carib, a light, golden lager, is the market leader, with Stag a close second. Stag is somewhat sweeter and, as the name suggests, it is heavily promoted as a man's beer. Both are best drunk out of a bottle, although they are also available on tap.

The Caribbean has a colorful pirate history and the association of pirates and rum still resonates. Trinis drink copious amounts of rum, both dark (known as red rum) and white. Fernandes, Black Label, Old Oak, and Vat 19 are among the most popular brands. Trinis generally like to drink their rum neat or with water, but popular mixers are Coca-Cola, ginger, or coconut water with a splash of Angostura bitters. A rum-based punch using various blended local fruits or lime, syrup, and bitters topped off with ground nutmeg is also popular, as is a coffee-based liqueur, Mokatika

Whiskey tends to be the drink of choice among men in the upper echelons of Trinbagonian society. Like other established brands of spirits it is expensive and therefore has social cachet. Trinis are not big wine drinkers, although wine bars have recently begun appearing in Port of Spain, and again it is a more elitist drink. Wine is generally imported and, although there are some homemade wines, they are hard to find. Alcohol is available in bars, rum shops, hotels, supermarkets, and other shops with a license to sell liquor.

Cold Drinks
Coconut water is widely available, cheap, and a delicious, healthy, and refreshing way to quench your thirst in the heat. Coconut sellers with their trucks piled high are a common sight. On request vendors will take a cutlass and chop off the top of a coconut's outer shell, revealing a hole in which to insert a straw so you can drink the pure juice straight from the nut. Once you have supped, the vendor will chop the nut into two so you can then scoop out the jelly using a piece of the husk as a spoon. Bottled coconut water is sold in shops, supermarkets, and at sporting events, but it tends to deteriorate quickly and doesn't taste as nice as the drink instantly available from vendors. The

trick is to take a bottle to the vendor and ask him to chop open several nuts so you can fill it up with fresh coconut water.

Despite an abundance of fruit in the islands, surprisingly few fresh fruit juices mixed by hand are available. Fruit juices, as well as Coca-Cola and Sprite, tend to be manufactured and are often heavily sugared. As with coconuts, there are plenty of orange sellers who will peel the fruit and cut them in half for you to eat.

Tea and Coffee

Trinis are tea drinkers, but they tend to drink it sweet and made with evaporated milk and sometimes even condensed milk. It's wisest to ask for tea without sugar if that's what you want. Failing that, don't stir your cup. Green tea is becoming increasingly popular but there is little interest in other herbal drinks, although they can be bought in supermarkets.

Considering that Trinidad and Tobago grows its own coffee, it's surprising to find that Trinis tend to drink instant coffee by well-known international brands. Like tea, coffee is usually served sweet, and it is only recently that a few cafés in major towns and at Trinidad's Piarco Airport and Tobago's Crown Point have begun to introduce variants such as lattes and cappuccinos. In rural areas, don't expect anything other than the instant variety.

EATING OUT

In towns, there are some very reasonable local places for lunch as most Trinis prefer a proper lunch, not a snack. In recent years, however, Port of Spain and the larger towns in Trinidad, as well as Scarborough and Crown Point in Tobago, have seen an increase in restaurant culture. Ariapita in Woodbrook in Port of Spain is considered the island's restaurant center, and most of Tobago's restaurants are in the touristy southwestern tip, Scarborough, and the northeast. Sit-down dining establishments in the mid-range and higher, with good, creative menus are scarce outside Port of Spain. Inevitably they are expensive, as are restaurants specializing in niche European food, such as

Italian or French. People come from all over Trinidad to San Fernando for halal meats barbequed over coals and served with garlic rolls, salad, and fries.

Traditional Creole fare is a mixture of provisions (pulses with root vegetables such as yams, cassava, and eddoes), and heavy-duty carbohydrates such as in macaroni pie and rice. Rice and dumplings are staples. Trinis are meat-lovers—chicken is the favorite—and Creole food does not therefore cater to vegetarians. But vegetarian options can be found in Indian food, as well as Chinese and Syrian, and the huge range of locally grown fruit and vegetables means vegetarians need never go hungry.

It's the younger generation who like eating out—families tend to eat at home. The big shopping malls all have food courts offering a wide range of local ethnic fare as well as international fast-food chains, including Kentucky Fried Chicken and Pizza Hut. The local food may be extremely good, but the constantly busy eating areas are usually designed to be purely functional, with fast service and little more than basic tables and chairs.

Street stalls sell everything from corn soup in polystyrene cups to plates of oysters, rotis, and doubles. Some might look uninviting, but don't be put off because they are generally hygienic and the vendors have to undergo regular hygiene checks before they are given official badge of approval. Word of mouth and recommendations will tell you which are the best to buy from.

Tobago's restaurants tend to offer a wider variety of food than Trinidad's, including steak imported from America, because they cater more to tourists. Prices are correspondingly higher.

Diners should be aware that the final bill will include a tax of up to 15 percent and normally a service charge of 10 percent. If the service charge is included, there's no need to leave a tip.

TIPPING

Tipping is not something that is widely practiced. As we've seen, most restaurants include a 10 percent service charge in the bill, which is usually split equally between all the waiters and waitresses. So if you want to tip someone in particular for exceptional service, make sure you hand them the cash rather than add it onto the bill or credit card payment.

Since most taxis are shared with other passengers being dropped off at fixed points along a route, tipping is not expected by the driver and to do so would draw unnecessary attention to yourself. To tip the driver of a privately hired taxi would, however, be the norm. Usually TT$5 or $TT10 (80 cents or US$1.60) would be sufficient, depending on the length of the journey.

Grocery packers in supermarkets do not expect a tip, but it is customary to give them a few dollars if they carry your bags of shopping to your car.

T&T's welfare system leaves a lot to be desired, but giving money to adult vagrant beggars is not encouraged. Small children are often to be found selling fruit on the beach and they can be given TT$1 or TT$2 even if you don't buy anything from them.

Table Manners
Until recently there was a relaxed attitude toward smoking, but it is now banned in all bars, restaurants, and clubs, and in public places.

Bread is not always eaten at every meal, but if eating a stew or dip, it is acceptable to use bread in place of cutlery, though not on business occasions. Stews and corn soup generally have dumplings and provisions in them so bread is not required.

If you're invited out for a meal it is polite to offer to pay when the bill arrives, but an invitation to dine out usually means you are being treated and you can therefore accept graciously. It is courteous to return the invitation.

SPORTS
Sport plays an important part in the islands' culture. A wide range of sports is taught and encouraged in school from an early age and the coverage in the newspapers reflects the Trini enthusiasm for every kind of sporting activity, major and minor, from cricket and football to squash and sailing.

Cricket
Trinbagonians are passionate about cricket; their appetite for the game borders on obsession. Makeshift games of cricket are to be found in progress on beaches, parks, and backstreets, and all over Trinidad's central Queen's Park Savannah as well as on more formal, established playing fields.

In the Queen's Park Oval, Port of Spain boasts the biggest and probably the most picturesque cricket ground in the whole of the Caribbean. It

is situated in Woodbrook, in the heart of Trinidad's capital, and from behind the Media Center stand the northern hills rise up to provide a glorious backdrop at one end of the ground.

Given a facelift for the 2007 cricket World Cup, the Queen's Park Oval has a proud history dating back to 1896. Through the years Trinidad and Tobago has regularly contributed star players to the West Indies international team, none more famous than Brian Lara, universally acknowledged as one of the best batsmen ever. He holds the record for the highest individual First Class score of 501, and the highest individual Test score of 400, records that are unlikely to be beaten. For twenty years until his retirement in 2007, Lara was feted as the Prince of Trinidad, and his standing as an all-time great has helped to inspire the current generation of players and to promote cricket generally in the two islands.

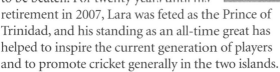

Interest in the traditional international five-day Test Match version of cricket has waned, but the 25,000 capacity ground is packed with excited, vocal spectators for the one-day internationals and Twenty20 matches, which usually take place in March and April. A noisy, colorful, highly partisan, carnival atmosphere pervades the crowd, and the liveliest area of the ground is the Trini Posse stand, where a ticket buys you not only a seat but all the food and drink you want, as well as a close-up view of scantily clad dancing girls who go through noisy liquid-limbed routines when a batsman hits a six or a wicket falls.

Victories over England, their old masters, are cause for the wildest celebrations of all. Matches are also followed avidly via live coverage on TV and on radio in offices, banks, shops, and bars. In Tobago, Scarborough's Shaw Park hosts regional first-class cricket fixtures.

Football

Football (soccer) is increasingly popular thanks in part to Trinidad and Tobago's national team making it through to the finals of the 2006 World Cup, the smallest English-speaking nation ever to qualify for the tournament. The Soca Warriors performed creditably, and major international matches at the National Stadium in Port of Spain now attract a fanatical following. There is healthy competition among the eleven teams that form the only professional league in the Caribbean and there is even a Women's League.

The profile of the sport has also been raised in recent years by a number of Trinbagonians achieving success at the top of England's Premier League—and acquiring the great wealth that goes with it. Most notable among them is Dwight Yorke, who became a hugely popular goalscorer for arguably the world's most famous club, Manchester United. Tobago now boasts a 7,500-capacity Dwight Yorke stadium at Bacolet near the capital, Scarborough.

Other Sports

Basketball, hockey, and rugby are all gaining in popularity, the latter due partly to the Armitage brothers Delon and Steffon playing rugby for England. Santa Rosa Park in Arima is Trinidad's only horse racing track and there are about forty race days annually, all on public holidays or Saturdays. As befits two islands, water sports—including sailing, sportfishing, kayaking, and surfing—are all popular, and Tobago is a world-class diving location with more than sixty established dive sites.

Trinbagonians are fiercely loyal to, supportive of, and inspired by their sporting heroes who fly the flag on the world stage. In recent years, swimming, golf, and athletics have all benefited from individuals excelling in international competition. Trinidad has six golf courses and Tobago has two eighteen-hole championship courses. Although still very much an elitist sport, the game has received a lift from the high profile success of professional golfer Stephen Ames. George Bovell III single-handedly managed much the same impact for swimming when he won a bronze medal at the 2004 Olympic Games in Athens. And as we've seen, Trini-born brothers Delon and Steffon Armitage recently gave rugby a shot in the arm by winning caps for England at rugby.

T&T is a nation that loves to run, and there are forty-five athletic clubs nationwide with competitive events held throughout the year. Athletics has received a massive boost from the emergence in the last decade of world-class sprinters Ato Boldon and Richard Thompson, who each won the silver medal in the 100 meters in the 2000 and 2008 Olympic Games respectively. They followed in the flying footsteps of Trinidad's first-ever Olympic gold medalist, Hasely Crawford, who won the 100 meters in Montreal in 1976. The national stadium in Port of Spain is referred to as the Hasely Crawford stadium.

OUT OF TOWN

On national holidays and at weekends, Trinis and Tobagonians head for the coast and a day at the beach or attend one of many fetes where there will be an entry fee for a day and/or a night of feasting, drinking, and dancing to live bands. In Trinidad, those who can afford them head for beachfront homes at Mayaro on the east coast of the island, where there are miles of deserted and unspoiled beaches.

River limes are especially popular among the Indian population. These usually begin in the early morning and see families set off for rural river locations to picnic, swim in the rivers, and laze on the banks, usually accompanied by loud music on a portable sound system. Cooking a meal on the banks of a river is an ongoing tradition and river limes go on until the late evening and even late into the night. River limes are so popular that even corporate events and parties are held beside a favorite river. Some rivers are lime-friendly, with stands and stools of bamboo, and metal huts or thatched-roof ajoupas to shelter in.

Hiking is popular on both islands, with an abundance of trails to be followed through tracts of forest to peaks, rivers, and waterfalls.

For Trinidadians, a flight to much quieter Tobago is always a popular option. Wealthier Trinis and the sailing set favor heading "down de islands." This refers to any of the collection of islands off the northwest coast of Trinidad: Five Islands, Gaspar Grande, and the Bocas Islands, five tiny islands in the Gulf of Paria. Boats are available for rental to spend the day sailing around in the sunshine and taking in the scenery of Gaspar Grande (also known as Gasparee), Chacachacare, Monos, Huevos, and Gasparillo. All these islands boast vacation homes—some lavish—and several of which are available for short-term rental.

In Trinidad, lifeguards are on duty from 9:00 a.m. to 5:00 p.m. or from 10:00 a.m. to

6:00 p.m. where available, but not at all beaches. Red flags indicate unsafe bathing areas. Trinidad's flagship beach Maracas Bay is undergoing an upgrade due to be completed in September 2011 to include a children's play area, zoned areas for sports, an event area for shows, a timber boardwalk, and elevation of the parking garage to counter the problem of flooding.

Foreigners should steer clear of the beaches in Chaguaramas, Galeota, and the areas between Point Lisas and Point Fortin. They may look inviting but can be contaminated by local industry.

For such a small island, Tobago has a remarkable number of events to attract and entertain visitors, tourists and locals alike. They include an Underwater Carnival (Dive Festival), a kite-flying festival, several food and culinary festivals, a two-week Heritage Festival, and an international drumming festival. The end of July ushers in the Great Fete weekend, which is in fact

not a weekend but a week of beach parties featuring the most popular DJs and sound systems, comprising Welcome Wednesday, Retro Thursday, Fantastic Friday, Wet Fete Saturday, Insomniac Sunday, and Bar Code Monday.

MUSIC

It's impossible to overstate how important music is to the people of Trinidad and Tobago. Music is an essential part of the culture; it plays a prominent role at religious ceremonies and in prayer as well as at any form of festival, celebration, or special family gathering. Its everyone-can-join-in appeal is eagerly and widely embraced from an early age.

Calypso

Trinbagonians all have a love for calypso (or kaiso) and are well versed in the proud history of this musical genre, which matches clever social commentary to music. Calypso has its roots in African folk songs, and over several hundred years it evolved first into a way of spreading news around Trinidad and then into the national musical genre of Trinidad and Tobago. The first calypso recording in 1914 raised the genre to a new level of popularity and paved the way for the establishment of "calypso tents" where calypsonians practiced and performed. This eventually led to the creation of famous stars like Lord Kitchener (Aldwin Roberts), Growling Tiger (Neville Marcano), and the Mighty Sparrow

(Slinger Francisco), all arch exponents of subtle
rhymes. With the use of clever lyrics, calypsonians
conjure up "picong"—songs of protest and satire
to poke fun at politicians, to pinpoint injustices,
to prick the consciences of wrongdoers, to
highlight controversial social topics, and to make
wry and amusing observations about island life.
The calypsos are usually sung by a solo singer
accompanied by a small downbeat backing band
and chorus singers ready to echo the most
poignant words and phrases. The annual climax
for calypsonians is the crowning of the Calypso
Monarch at Carnival.

Pan
Trinidad and Tobago can claim to the distinction
of having invented the only new acoustic musical
instrument in the twentieth century: the steel pan.
Today people on every continent are acquainted
with pan, as Trinis simply call it. But while this
musical genre wins rave reviews in performances
at the Sydney Opera House, London's Royal Albert
Hall, and New York's Carnegie Hall, the land of its

birth remains the mecca of pan. To the uninitiated, it's a mystery how an amalgamation of percussion instruments made from discarded oil drums can correctly interpret music originally composed for conventional string and wind instruments.

The Well-tempered Steel Pan
Pans are cut to size and the unopened ends are pounded by a 5-pound (2.3-kg) hammer. They are then placed on a fire for forty minutes before oil is thrown over them to temper the steel. A coating of chrome gives the pan a smoother surface and a sparkling finish. The required notes are marked on the surface before a tuner sets to work with a hammer and chisel.

The Steel Band
The steel band developed from the banning, many years ago, on Carnival days of the tamboo-bamboo drum bands, who used pieces of bamboo

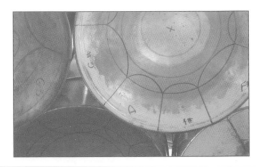

cut to different lengths to form primitive
percussive kalinda music to accompany stick
fighting. The authorities had a fear of primitive
rhythms, decided the bands' drumbeats had a
disturbing influence on Carnival celebrations,
and banned them. But in 1937 a band from New
Town swept noisily into Port of Spain on Carnival
Monday led by Lord Humbugger, wearing just a
top hat and black overcoat. Ostensibly this band
was paying tribute to the hit film of the day,
Alexander's Ragtime Band, and had a banner
proclaiming this. But this was a band born of the
city slums and they beat out their electrifying
rhythms with steel rods on dustbin lids,
saucepans, buckets, and the hubcaps and brake
drums of automobiles and other bits of steel. It
proved an infectious rallying call to the revelers
who joined in with unbridled enthusiasm to enjoy
the beat—and the steel band was born.

The sound was significantly augmented after
the Second World War by adapting old oil drums
discarded or abandoned by the American GIs
based in Trinidad. Trinis quickly discovered the

oil drums could be hammered into concave sections to produce a variety of musical notes.

As the bands came from the poorer districts and had such threatening names as Invaders and Desperadoes, band members were regarded as "bad johns" and Trinidad's steel bands became associated with a period of violence. Running feuds were common among the rival panyards that sprang up in the deprived areas. The feuding climaxed in a bloody clash between Invaders and Tokyo on Carnival Tuesday in 1956, which was immortalized in a famous calypso by Lord Blakie called "The Steelband Clash."

Gradually, as pan became more widely accepted and the music more intricate and sophisticated, the link with violence diminished and led to the formation of the T&T Steelband Association, now called Pan Trinbago. The first Panorama tournament was staged in 1963 and the steel pan was officially declared the national instrument by the then prime minister, Eric Williams.

Today the government encourages major companies to sponsor bands. Some years ago it was realized that sponsorship helped to eliminate the violent gang element among steel bands because sponsors would back out if bands fought.

Bands consist of anything up to two hundred volunteers forming huge symphonic pan orchestras. To appreciate their talent fully you must hear them live and in the open air. Vinyl and CD recordings have never been able to capture adequately the remarkable sound of a large band in full swing. In the run up to Panorama, you can catch for free the bands practicing in their various panyards.

Ping Pong or Soprano pans, with up to thirty-two notes, take the lead to produce the melody, while behind them are the harmony sections—alto, tenor, guitar, cello, and bass pans—a rhythm section with drums, cymbals, and scratchers, and the iron men beating out the rhythm.

There are many who maintain that a steel band should restrict itself to music composed only for pan. But the remarkable fact is that a steel band with pans of all ranges and depths, lovingly created by pan tuners, can interpret everything from Gershwin's *Jazz Concerto* to Beatles' numbers to Holst's *The Planets* and other classical masterpieces by the great composers.

The annual climax of every pan player's year is Panorama, a February event attracting upward of 25,000 people who flock to see and hear T&T's top bands compete on a stage erected on Port of Spain's Savannah, after winning their regional heats. Other major pan events include the World Steel Band Festival, usually held in October, Pan Ramajay in May, and the Pan Jazz Festival in November.

Soca

Soca, short for soul calypso, is a modern form of beefed up calypso dance music driven along with an insistent, often electronic, beat. Its origins date back to 1973, when Trinidad's Lord Shorty (born Garfield Blackman) began writing calypso songs with structured rhythms more suited to get-up-and-dance party music and which sat easily alongside the emergence of disco music at the time. The genre has spawned a plethora of local acts who fuse Africa-derived calypso with exciting East Indian rhythms. They come into their own in the run-up to Carnival. In January the soca artistes release their new CDs at major launches where they showcase their new material, which in turn become the hot new numbers to dance to at the ensuing Carnival fetes. Along with the new party music come new dance routines, which rapidly spread among soca fans. Soca has gained such popularity over the past twenty years that there is now a Soca

Monarch competition, an event contested by dozens of homegrown artistes and attended by vast numbers of people. Soca has become the form of music most preferred by revelers during Carnival, and Trinidad and Tobago's national football team are known as the Soca Warriors.

Chutney Soca

As the name suggests, this is crossover soca music, flavored with a blend of Hindi and English lyrics, allied to East Indian instruments including the sitar and dholak drums. It's enjoyed primarily by young East Indians but important enough in T&T's musical fabric for the National Chutney Soca Monarch to be staged annually for the past sixteen years, usually in San Fernando.

Rapso

Don't be misled into believing rapso is logically the fusion of American rap with soca music. In fact, rapso is a unique T&T style of politically aware street poetry that originated in the 1970s, when the twin islands were experiencing political upheaval and unrest and the trade unions were making a stand. Rapso emerged as a way to relate to the everyday experiences of ordinary people, and some of the first rapso songs were chanted by striking workers on the picket lines. In the 1990s a new generation of rapso artistes emerged, adding dance rhythms and hip-hop influences to lyrics spoken in a calypso style but with an American rap urgency. With the help of niche fetes and specific CDs, they further popularized the musical genre to the extent that there is now a rapso month staged in April or May at venues across Port of Spain.

Reggae

A big increase in the number and popularity of local reggae performers reflects the growing appeal of this form of music, particularly among the young. Due to interisland rivalry, the older generation still tends to regard reggae as inferior music from Jamaica. Known as dub by Trinis, reggae music has also had an influence on soca.

Parang

As we have seen, parang is a Spanish-flavored style of folk music and T&T's version of carol singing. It is one of the last celebrated links back to the Spanish colonization of Trinidad. Parang comes into its own during the Christmas season when the *paranderos* rove from house to house in the neighborhood serenading families and friends. In exchange for the entertainment they are given food and drink.

The bands consist of four to six singers with musicians on guitar, mandolin, violin, cello, bandol, box bass, maracas, claves, marimbola, tambourine, scratchers, and cuatro—a small four-stringed guitar. Traditional parang lyrics were mainly religious and the songs were sung in Spanish, as they still are today. In recent years soca and calypso have also fused with parang to create soca-parang, featuring songs with English lyrics.

CINEMA

Trinidad and Tobago may seem too small to have much of a cinema tradition, but Trinidadians have been cinemagoers ever since the first movie house was established in 1911. And it was important enough by the late 1930s for Humphrey Bogart to fly into Port of Spain to be given the red carpet treatment to open the Deluxe Cinema. Both islands were used as locations during Hollywood's golden age for movies such as *Affair in Trinidad* in 1952, starring Rita Hayworth and Glenn Ford, *Heaven Knows, Mr. Allison* in 1957, with Robert Mitchum and Deborah Kerr, and *Fire Down Below* in 1957 with Mitchum and Hayworth.

The Trinidad and Tobago Film Company is dedicated to the film industry in the two islands. The TTFC helps to fund nationals and permanent residents wanting to make films and documentaries and there are currently around a dozen production companies employing a core staff of two hundred. There are an additional thirty companies offering production support. The TTFC recently introduced a rebate program in a bid to attract international filmmakers to make use of T&T's geographical beauty as film locations. Under this incentive, producers and production companies can claim cash rebates of up to 30 percent for expenditure incurred while filming in the islands. No fewer than four films were being made around Carnival in 2010, all four productions facilitated by the TTFC.

T&T also stages a well-attended annual film festival featuring movies made by Caribbean people, by persons of the Caribbean Diaspora, and by international filmmakers who have made movies that reflect Caribbean cultures and way of life. Each September the festival showcases drama movies, documentaries, short and animated films from or about the Caribbean and Latin America, and hosts workshops and educational programs.

Trinbagonians like going to the cinema, especially now that the big American-style state-of-the-art multiscreen complexes have largely replaced the old-time fleapits. The modern complexes are to be found in shopping malls in Port of Spain, in suburban Trincity and Chaguanas. They show all the latest Hollywood movies soon after they have been released in the USA. In outlying areas there are a handful of older established movie houses, some of which show predominantly Indian Bollywood films. Trinidad's film buffs can see foreign films and fringe cinema free of charge through the Studio Film Club.

After decades without a cinema, Tobago finally welcomed the arrival of a multiscreen Movietowne center, which opened in 2008.

Moviegoing is an event, and at the Movietowne cinema complexes audiences on both islands are encouraged to take in drinks and food on a tray that slots into the arm-rest of a seat. Going to the cinema can also be a noisy experience. Don't be surprised if audiences are vocal, dishing out advice to the various screen characters, making fun of others, and offering the occasional line to the plot. Hollywood's usually distorted vision of the Caribbean and its people may be greeted with catcalls of derision. The credits at the end of a movie seem to be of no interest to patrons, who head for the exits as soon as a movie ends.

All movies are subject to T&T's censorship and scenes of excessive violence, gratuitous sex, and anything considered blasphemous will be cut out.

Visitors should also be aware that sitting through a two-hour film at Movietowne can be an uncomfortably chilly experience. The management tends to turn up the air-conditioning to shiver level, which contrasts sharply with the sunny heat you basked in before walking into the cinema.

THEATER

The theater scene inevitably takes second place to Carnival, but the Trinidad Theatre Workshop, founded in 1959 by the 1992 Nobel Laureate Derek Walcott, produces quality,  original plays as well as works by a wide range of established, well-known dramatists ranging from Tennessee Williams to Neil Simon.

Although Trinis are not great theatergoers, other small drama groups manage to thrive in Trinidad, but much less so in Tobago. Commercial productions are usually popular farces, either locally originated or adaptations of foreign plays. Trinidad's festivals usually produce both original and ritual drama based on traditions and folklore.

SHOPPING FOR PLEASURE

Port of Spain is the best place to shop. Most notably it has a wide selection of shops selling fabrics, from exotic batiks and sari silks to men's suits and fine linens. Souvenirs to seek out include jewelry influenced by East Indian and Venezuelan designers, local paintings, prints, sculpture, pottery, ceramics, wind chimes, mosaics, metal sculpture, calabash and coconut jewelry and vessels, handmade soaps, and locally made leather sandals, bags, and belts.

Increasingly, American-style multilevel malls have become the focal point for shopping in Trinidad and Tobago. There are around twenty-five shopping malls throughout the two islands and Trincity Mall, thirty minutes from Port of Spain and ten minutes from Piarco Airport, is one of the largest malls in the southern Caribbean with more than two hundred stores. The big towns have malls ranging in size from a hundred shops upward, offering services from supermarkets to boutiques, pharmacies to luxury goods, as well as entertainment (cinemas and bars). Most stores accept major credit cards or US currency as well as the $TT.

The Trinidad and Tobago (TT) dollar comes in coins of 1 cent, 5 cents, 10 cents, and 25 cents. Notes are in denominations of $1, $5, $10, $20, and $100. American dollars are generally acceptable but exchange rates are subject to fluctuation. Except for 15 percent Value Added Tax (VAT) imposed on the sticker price of some goods and services, no additional exit duties are placed on goods.

Younger Trinbagonians treat a visit to the malls as a social outing, where they can meet up with their friends in air-conditioned comfort, window-shop, and sit down to have a refreshing drink, a meal in the food courts, and see the latest Hollywood movie at the multiplex cinema.

Away from these suburban shopping centers, main streets in the major towns also have arcades and small variety shops. Family-run businesses flourish in mini-marts, and roadside and street vending is also extremely common. Everything from fruit and vegetables to mad bulls (large kites) are available from a tray on the sidewalk, from a cart, or from the back of a pickup truck.

On weekends, many locals get up early to visit one of a number of Trinidad's street markets and bazaars, which open from 6:00 a.m. selling fruit and vegetables, fresh meat, and live chickens. Central Market at Sea Lots in Port of Spain is the largest, but smaller towns and villages, Sangre Grande in particular, also have lively markets where goods are cheap and farm fresh.

In Tobago it is worth noting the location of the main supermarkets because, although every village has one or more small local shops, they tend to stock only basic goods, the range of commodities is small, and many staple goods are sold only in large economy sizes. All the supermarkets accept payment by credit card but require some sort of photo identity so take a passport.

In neither Trinidad nor Tobago is bargaining customary. You will be considered rude if you try to haggle, especially if it is over something inexpensive like local craft. If you want to bargain in such a situation, do so only if you really intend to buy. It is best to pay cash for items sold at markets and bazaars; otherwise you may be charged more.

In Tobago, the Gulf City Lowlands Mall is a one-stop commercial center for shopping and is located just off the highway between Crown Point and Scarborough. Lower Scarborough has a smaller mall.

FASHION

Thanks to Carnival, Trinbagonians have always enjoyed dressing up and there is a thriving culture of design, dressmaking, and sewing. This has given rise to a healthy fashion industry with close to sixty fashion houses and an abundance of creative and technical talent showcased annually during a well respected fashion week. Inevitably clothing design is based on ethnicity, and fabric stores to suit all styles can be found throughout Trinidad. Queen and Frederick Streets in downtown Port of Spain are considered the best places to buy textiles, Indian silks, and other materials. Some shops have a vast inventory of fabric for all occasions, while others specialize in high-end material for weddings, special events, and drapery.

In Trinidad there are a number of designers and fashion houses, some of them respected internationally, like Claudia Pegus, Heather Jones, Meiling, Millhouse, Radical Designs, and The Cloth. These designers have retail outlets or ateliers where you can purchase their work. Many Trinis are of course *au fait* with all the latest fashions from America because the shops are full of popular US brands of clothing, particularly casual wear for the young—jeans, T-shirts, sneakers, fashionable tops, and skirts.

ECOTOURISM

Trinidad and Tobago receives around 250,000 tourists each year from January to July, when the climate is at its most temperate. While Tobago offers unspoiled beaches, picturesque bays, all manner of water sports, charming coastal villages, and small towns, the island is also rightly regarded as one of the top ecotourism destinations in the world, and it has a clutch of awards to prove it. Tobagonians are understandably proud that their island has the oldest legally protected rain forest in the world, dating back to 1776.

It was English scientist Stephen Hales who worked out the delicate link between forests and rainfall and that, if forests were cut down, rainfall would cease. But it took eleven years of campaigning by Soame Jenyns, an English MP friend of the scientist, to persuade the authorities that continual logging by the colonial plantation owners would eventually ruin Tobago. Success was achieved on April 13, 1776, when a law was passed protecting in perpetuity what is now known as the Main Ridge Forest Reserve, which runs along a mountainous ridge along the upper, eastern half of the island. Many even believe this law to be the world's first environmental act.

Birds

Around 220 species of birds have been recorded in Tobago, an astonishing number considering the island measures just 26 by 7 miles (42 by 10 km). They range from tanagers to mockingbirds, hummingbirds to woodpeckers. Together, Trinidad and Tobago have more bird species than the rest of the Caribbean combined.

Little Tobago and St. Giles, two little islands off the coast of Tobago, are world renowned for the seabird colonies that thrive on their windswept cliffs. Avid bird-watchers should note that landings are controlled for conservation purposes and you need a permit and a guide.

Little Tobago is just one mile (1.6 km) long and accessible only by boat from Speyside but worth it to see such rare birds as Brown Boobies, Red-billed Tropicbirds, Laughing Gulls, and  Audubon Shearwaters. Red-footed Boobies and Frigate Birds have been sighted on St. Giles.

Wildlife

The diverse South American flora and fauna that flourishes in Tobago also includes twenty-three species of butterfly, including the Blue Emperor (there are more than six hundred butterfly species in Trinidad). The wildlife also embraces raccoons, red squirrels, opossums, agoutis, wild pigs, armadillos, twenty-four species of nonpoisonous snakes, sixteen species of lizard, of which the largest is the Green Iguana, fourteen species of frog and seventeen species of bat, including a nocturnal fish-eating variety.

Coral Reefs

Tobago is fringed by some of the best reef formations in the Caribbean. The proximity of the island to South America places it in the path of the Guyana Current, which feeds the area with nutrients from the Orinoco River, thereby attracting a huge variety of marine life. Buccoo Reef is the island's largest and was designated a marine park in 1973. It comprises five flat reefs of Elkhorn coral, Brain coral, Starlet and Star corals. The reef can be enjoyed by glass-bottomed boat, but don't accept any plastic sandals that you may be offered or walk in any coral area as the slightest contact can damage or destroy the delicate organisms. Tobago's tropical climate makes diving possible all year-round with decent visibility up to 120 feet (40 m).

Giant Leatherbacks

Both Trinidad and Tobago are putting energy and
resources into conservation and protection of the
critically endangered giant leatherback turtles.
Weighing up to 1,540 lb (700 kg) and measuring
up to 13 feet (4 m across), the females drag
themselves up on to T&T's secluded beaches to
excavate nests in the sand in which to lay their eggs.
These turtles swim thousands of miles in order to
return to the beach where they were born in order
to lay their eggs. In the months between March and
June every year, T&T's northern beaches become a
leatherback maternity home and a nursery to
thousands of hatchlings some fifty-five to seventy
days later. The female turtles emerge from the
waves only at night and struggle laboriously and
slowly up beach inclines to dig holes with their rear
flippers in soft sand, into which they drop up to
eighty eggs at a time. The whole natural process,
which can take up to two hours, is an awe-
inspiring, unforgettable experience not to be
missed, particularly the
extraordinary sight of
the female appearing
to weep as she strains
to lays her eggs. In
fact the "tears" she
copiously secretes are

to keep her eyes clear of sand and sea salt
while she is out of the water.

As the turtles come ashore only under cover of
darkness, the beaches are patrolled by guards in the
egg laying season to ensure the leatherbacks are

untroubled by lights, camera flashes, noisy human approaches, or excitable children trying to ride on their backs. The protection patrols are concerned citizens called the Nature Seekers, who have won many ecotourism awards since their inception in 1990. The patrols know exactly the right moments to switch on small flashlights to allow small groups of visitors a clear view of the remarkable spectacle without disturbing the turtles. As dawn comes up there are usually enough leatherback latecomers still laying or painstakingly using their flippers to cover up their nests with sand to allow plenty of time for photographs.

Green and hawksbill sea turtles also nest in Tobago as well as leatherbacks, and visitors can help protect all three species by not selling or purchasing sea turtle products.

Swamp Life

The Caroni swamp is Trinidad's prized bird sanctuary and well worth a visit if only to watch a spectacular flyover by a flock of Trinidad's national bird, the magnificent long-billed Scarlet Ibis. You have to take a boat tour to visit the swamp; this begins with a boatman steering carefully along natural canals dividing the densely packed, twisted roots of mangrove trees. On either side the roots are crawling with tree-climbing fiddler crabs, while the occasional swamp boa curls around branches overhead. Out in the lagoon, the boatman selects a stationary point some distance away from a mangrove island so as not to disturb the Scarlet Ibis as they come home to roost each evening on their return from Venezuela to feed. Right on cue, shortly before dusk, the flock of Scarlet Ibis wing their way gracefully through the sky toward the island's green mangrove branches ready for the night. They are a wonderful sight, their magnificent scarlet plumage gained from the ingestion of red crabs in the tropical swamps, which gradually turns their feathers red from an initial gray and white.

The Asa Wright Centre
Foreigners on their first visit to Trinidad will either be invited, or urged, to visit (or better still to stay at) the Asa Wright Nature Centre located 1,200 feet (370 m) up in the mountains of the Northern Range, seven miles to the north of the town of Arima. Back in 1947 Icelandic naturalist and bird lover Asa and her husband bought the former coffee-cocoa-citrus plantation and when he died she sold the land with the proviso it remained a conservation area. Now the Wrights' former home, a beautifully remodeled colonial estate house nearly a hundred years old, is the centerpiece of this 198-acre (80-ha) nature retreat. The house's veranda overlooking the Arima valley is famously a bird-watcher's paradise with an array of exotic and brilliantly colored birds drawn to the feeders thoughtfully sited for visitors at eye level just yards away. The Asa Wright Centre is a two-hour drive from Port of Spain and it's wise to get there early to avoid the rush. There are tours of the lush flower-filled grounds along forest trails led by guides with expert knowledge of the teeming wildlife, flora, and fauna.

chapter seven

TRAVEL, HEALTH, & SAFETY

Trinidad and Tobago's transport infrastructure is no more than adequate and is poorly maintained. Most Trinbagonians get around by car and every journey is an obstacle course. There are no trains, and public transportation consists of crowded buses that may, or may not, have air-conditioning and may or may not be on time. Long-distance bus journeys are usually comfortable and entertaining, however, rather than alarming, with much chatter and convivial sharing of food and drink.

INTERISLAND TRAVEL

The easiest and fastest way to travel between Trinidad and Tobago is by plane with Caribbean Airlines. There are a dozen daily flights between Trinidad's Piarco Airport, which is 17 miles (27 km) from Port of Spain and Tobago's Crown Point Airport, which is 7 miles (10 km) from Scarborough. These regular flights run more or less on time between 6:00 a.m. and 10:00 p.m. but they are liable to be overbooked. If traveling from Tobago to Trinidad around Carnival time, the service may well be oversubscribed. Similar problems may be encountered when traveling

from Trinidad to Tobago at peak periods,
including the latter's Easter weekend, the
Plymouth Jazz Festival in April, and the Great
Race weekend in August. Even if you are clutching
a confirmed ticket you may experience delays. The
subsidized airfare costs $TT150 (about US$24,
£10) one way and $TT 300 round-trip. Internet
bookings are now available. You don't need a
passport if you've already been through
immigration on either island but visitors always
need ID so one might as well take it.

The slower alternative is to travel by ferry.
There are two fast ferries operating between
Trinidad and Tobago catering to 800 passengers

and up to 250 cars. The journey time is two and a half hours. A standard ferry takes twice as long but is the cheapest way to travel between the islands. The crossing by conventional ferry takes between five and six hours but it can be rough. The cost of taking a car is based on the type, model, size, and weight of the vehicle. Tickets are not available for purchase online but can be bought at the Government Shipping Service Terminal, Wrightson Road, Port of Spain, or at selected TTPost outlets. In Tobago tickets are purchased at the Tobago Terminal Office on Carrington Street in Scarborough. Tickets should be bought at least three hours before the ferry departs to avoid waiting in line.

LOCAL TRANSPORTATION
Public transportation consists of buses and Maxi taxis. Buses are used mainly by the working classes and people who cannot afford a car. Middle-class and wealthy Trinis very rarely use public transportation, preferring to drive, particularly as the size of the island means no journey is too far or takes up too much time behind the wheel.

Intercity Travel
With no trains, there are few options for intercity travel within the islands. If visiting outlying rural areas, renting a car is by far the best option. A rental car is also advisable if you go out late at night because, although public transportation does run all night in Port of Spain and San

Fernando, it is more intermittent than during the day and it stops around midnight elsewhere. Public buses can be erratic and very crowded at peak times, so the best way to get around without a rental car is to use the network of Maxi taxis, route taxis, or private taxis.

Although there are no trains at present, a billion-dollar Rapid Rail system is proposed for Trinidad with seventeen stations along 60 miles (98 km) of parallel double track railway. The rail network will serve the East–West corridor between Westmoorings in Port of Spain and Sangre Grande, and the North–South corridor between Curepe and San Fernando. The plan is for the network to be built in five segments and eventually link Port of Spain, Chaguanas, San Fernando, Curepe, Arima, and Sangre Grande.

Maxi Taxis

Maxi taxis are privately owned minibuses carrying between ten and twenty people that travel along set routes with set fares. Maxis are distinguishable by the letter H (for hire) on their vehicle registration plate and color-coded stripes denote in which area of Trinidad they operate. Yellow stripes indicate Maxis running from Port of Spain to the western end of Trinidad. Red stripes signify operation along an eastern route from Port of Spain to Sangre Grande. Maxis with green stripes ply the Port of Spain to Chaguanas route to the center and the south; black stripes cover the southern parts of the island and from Chaguanas to Princes Town; and brown stripes operate between San Fernando and communities on the southwest peninsula.

Maxis start out from main centers. To be sure of a seat it's best to go to these main stands, where the Maxi driver will wait until his bus is full before setting off. At the press of a passenger's buzzer, to be found near the window, the driver can be asked to stop at any point along the route to allow someone off. A Maxi can be hailed with a wave of the hand anywhere along its route and, provided there is space, the driver will stop to pick you up. Before you get on, ask the driver to confirm which route he is traveling. Bear in mind that some Maxis on popular routes at busy times may be full from starting point to destination.

Because they are privately owned, Maxis operate with no specific timetable but there are plenty of them around during the busy morning and evening periods. At night they are less frequent. Be prepared for drivers to veer off the route occasionally to pick up more passengers and, if the Maxi is full from the start, the driver may choose to take a shorter, more direct route to his destination.

Similarly, on request, Maxis may take a short detour to set you down at an off-route point, but it's at the discretion of the driver and you may be asked to pay a little extra for the favor. Be aware that your journey may be accompanied by the playing of loud music if you board a Maxi that has a license to do so. Fares are fixed and go up only when there's a rise in gas prices. The rates are not displayed but journeys are cheap. Locals usually know what to pay. Inquire at your hotel or ask a friend what the fare is.

In Tobago, Scarborough to Charlotteville is the only set route and this is operated by blue-striped Maxis. Other Maxis are privately rented by tourists.

Route Taxis

Route taxis are cars that operate a similar sort of system to the Maxi taxis. They are distinguishable by the letter H on their number plate. They are licensed to take a maximum of five passengers and they will not set off from their stands until they are full, which means you may be kept waiting for a while. They are generally quicker than Maxi taxis because they make fewer drop-off stops, but they may also be less comfortable as people climb in laden with bags of shopping or personal luggage.

As with Maxis, route taxis will stop at the wave of a hand and local practice is to point which direction you plan to take at the next major junction. It's polite to say "good morning" or "good afternoon" to the other passengers as you climb in. If your destination is off the stated route, you could try bargaining with the driver to make a detour provided the other passengers are agreeable. Crammed in with other people, you are bound to be engaged in conversation, with local and international politics a favorite topic.

Private Taxis

Private taxis can be hired from cab companies and will take you to your destination without stopping to pick up anyone else. They do not have meters so you must agree upon a price before embarking on your journey. Inevitably this door-to-door taxi service is very much more expensive than traveling by Maxi or route taxi.

Like Maxis and route taxis, private taxis will display the letter H on their number plate. Trade vehicles will display the letter T and privately owned cars have the letter P. However, there are some "pirate" P-registered cars operating as taxis illegally, mostly at night.

Women should in any case always try to sit in the back of the cab, rather than upfront with the driver, especially if they are traveling alone. Expect some cabs to be in shabby condition, with doors that don't close properly and windows that may not open or close. Most drivers now have cell phones so if you establish a rapport you can call them to arrange to be picked up and dropped off.

Buses

Bus travel has improved in recent years and is now a reasonable way of getting around in Trinidad and Tobago. Two public bus companies connect towns and villages in Trinidad: the Super Express blue transit bus line and the red, white, and black ECS bus line. Both operate from the City Gate terminus, also known as South Quay. Bus tickets in both islands must be bought in advance from either the main terminals or from stores, and weekly and monthly tickets are available. The newer buses are air-conditioned, some of them left over from a fleet commissioned for recent international conferences hosted by Trinidad's prime minister. Bus routes in Trinidad cover most of the island, but some of the more scenic coastal villages do not have a reliable service.

In Tobago, buses leave from the terminal at Greenside Street in Scarborough. Bus stops along the routes may consist of just a primitive roadside shelter or simply a small sign on a pole.

Trinidad's main bus terminal, City Gate, is located at South Quay, Port of Spain, and in Tobago a regular daily service throughout the island runs from the main bus terminal at Sangster's Hill, Scarborough. A special service runs from Crown Point International Airport every thirty minutes on weekdays and every hour on weekends. When using the bus service on either island it is advisable to confirm departure times as schedules can change without notice.

Water Taxi

In 2010 a water taxi service began operating from Port of Spain's docks to San Fernando across the Gulf of Paria and back. Parking is free at both ends and the journey takes about forty minutes.

DRIVING

Driving in Trinidad and Tobago is on the left and signs are in miles. Wording on the signs is often in Spanish as well as English.

Driving here is not for the fainthearted. Infinite patience is required behind the wheel as well as unwavering concentration and a general acceptance that every journey is likely to be an obstacle course. Watch out for bumpy roads, gaping potholes, sudden lane changing, turning without signaling, stray dogs, aggressive driving, unfamiliar hand signals, and a penchant for drivers to stop without warning.

It's not uncommon for traffic to grind to a halt simply because two drivers have stopped to lime. An unnerving disregard for authority and traffic regulations adds to the need for foreigners to stay alert. The speed limit in Trinidad is 80 kph (50 mph) on highways and 55 kph (34 mph) in built-up areas. In Tobago it's 50 kph (31mph). Speed limit signs written in kilometers. There are no left turns on red and U-turns are illegal.

"There are laws but they are all meant to be broken," Trinis are liable to say cheerfully, while insisting that they are all good drivers. They point out that the roads present so many hazards that the laws simply have to be disregarded. Speed limits are frequently ignored, and the use of police radar machines to catch speeding drivers is minimal.

The introduction of the breathalyzer in 2009 has reduced the chances of encountering drunk drivers on the road, but they remain a limited risk, particularly at night. Talking on a cell phone while driving is illegal but is rarely enforced.

The congested maze of one-way streets and pedestrian-packed sidewalks in Port of Spain, particularly in Independence Square, and in Scarborough in Tobago, can prove a challenge.

Trinidad's rush hours and the gridlocked roads in Port of Spain will tax even the most patient of drivers.

Two main multilane roads run from north to south and from east to west in Trinidad, and there is a major highway running west to east in Tobago. The main roads and highways are generally well maintained, but minor roads leave a lot to desired; some are so bad they deserve the Trini description of being "behind God's back."

Many rural roads wind their way through steep embankments, which makes night driving difficult. The twists and turns mean blind corners, and an added hazard are landslides following torrential rain. In Tobago, roads tend to be narrow and in rural areas drivers should look out for sheep and chickens, as well as stray dogs, possibly running into their path

Car Rental

An up-to-date international driving license is required for both cars and motorcycles, or a current driver's license from the UK, the USA, Canada, Germany, France, or the Bahamas. These are valid for up to ninety days after arrival, but for longer stays applications should be made to the Licensing Division. You must be able to produce your driver's license on the spot so make sure you take it with you. It's also advisable to have your insurance certificate with you in the car.

Car rental companies generally require drivers to be at least twenty-five years of age and to have two years' driving experience. The law requires drivers and both front and backseat passengers to wear seat belts. Failure to do so can result in one of the heaviest of driving fines. A points scheme is in operation for offenses, which can ultimately result in a loss of license.

Gas stations are plentiful in cities and towns on main thoroughfares throughout the country, but less so in rural areas, particularly in Tobago, where they are also likely to close much earlier. Gas is cheap by UK standards. Around $100TT (about US$16, or £10) will fill up the tank of an average size car.

It's said that no one gives directions quite like a Trinidadian. Ask for help to get to a certain place and advice will be freely given, mostly correctly. But sometimes, instead of admitting ignorance, in their willingness to please Trinis may send you on a route that's quite likely to get you lost. When giving directions there is also often confusion between left and right, and they are more likely to direct you via landmarks, and to use the word "swing" for turn.

Drivers should be particularly alert when driving behind vehicles with a number plate bearing the letter H. This, as we have seen, indicates the vehicle is a taxi, which is therefore liable to stop without warning at any time. Taxi drivers possess a confusing array of hand signals to indicate turning, stopping, or slowing, so slow down if you see any hand signal from an H-registered vehicle.

When leaving Port of Spain and heading toward Piarco Airport, take extra care not to stray by mistake on to the priority route for buses, taxis, and emergency vehicles only. This priority route runs parallel to the Churchill Roosevelt Highway from Port of Spain in the west to Arima in the east.

Accidents

In the event of an accident, write down the name, address, and insurance details of the driver involved and inform the police to make a report. It's a good idea to take your own photos of the accident if possible and of your own witnesses if necessary. Trinidad and Tobago are small islands and, as the police may often know the locals involved, the tendency is to favor those with whom they are familiar. Uninsured drivers, of which there are many, generally sort out their own terms and remuneration if they are involved in a collision in which there is no physical damage.

Parking

Parking meters have yet to arrive in Trinidad, and parking in the major towns can be thoroughly confusing. Often parking will be permitted on one side of the street on one day and on the other side of the same street on another day. Since Trinis tend not to take much notice of these restrictions, it can be difficult working out on which side it is legitimate to park your car on any given day. Check the parking signs carefully or you may find yourself towed away. Port of Spain and other big towns have multistory parking garages, and yards designated for parking with attendants who may be difficult to spot because they don't wear uniforms. Because the streets tend to be narrow in towns, it's important to park legally to allow traffic to flow freely and to avoid double parking, even if other drivers indulge. All the major shopping malls and supermarkets provide parking free of charge.

PEDESTRIANS

As with drivers, pedestrians need to be vigilant at all times as the sidewalks in towns tend to be narrow, uneven, and potholed, and you're liable to come across a variety of obstacles—from old oil drums to litter, to street markets—encroaching across them. Getting across the multilaned road that surrounds Port of Spain's Savannah can be hazardous simply because of the seemingly ceaseless heavy flow of traffic. Here it is wisest to cross at designated pedestrian crossings, which drivers do respect.

WHERE TO STAY
Hotels

Trinidad and Tobago both have accommodation to suit every pocket. Port of Spain has a number of flagship hotels, including a recently revamped Hilton, with high-tech amenities, executive lounges, laptop rental, and twenty-four-hour fully equipped business and presentation editing centers. When quoted a room rate, check whether it includes not only breakfast but also the 10 percent Hotel Accommodation Tax and the service charge, which may also be an additional 10 percent. Trinidad's hotels and guesthouses are chiefly located in Port of Spain. There are also hotels in the San Fernando and outlying areas serving the industrialized south of the island and the central regions, including Point Fortin, Point Lisas, and Chaguanas. New hotels have also recently sprung up close to Piarco International Airport.

For tourists exploring Trinidad accommodation is available in Grande Riviere, the Arima Valley, Salybia, Mount St. Benedict, Blanchisseuse, and Chaguaramas. Bookings should be made well in advance of Carnival and major conferences.

Tobago is far more tourist-oriented than Trinidad and accommodation ranges from luxury hotels, beachfront villas, and B&Bs to ecolodges, dive lodges, and guesthouses. When booking, bear in mind the Crown Point area is the hub of activities—tourist information, Republic Bank, hotels, apartments, car, jeep and bike rentals, restaurants, and historic Fort Milford.

Apartments

Finding an apartment in either island is simple. In Trinidad the daily newspapers list apartments to rent and some are advertised online. Unless you are thoroughly familiar with the areas advertised, however, it is best to go through estate agents, who can advise you on which areas to avoid, either because they have a high incidence of crime or because they are not easily accessible. It is important to establish a good relationship with your agent and sensible to ask him or her to accompany you to view an apartment.

Short lets of a week or two are uncommon except during Carnival or when Trinidad is hosting a Test Match in Port of Spain. Prices may be much higher during Carnival.

Most apartments will be furnished and if it is not to your taste the landlord can be persuaded to store the furniture. The two most important questions to address are whether the apartment is clean and whether it is safe. With the huge increase in crime, gated complexes are advisable. Many apartments have protective grilles over windows to discourage forced entry, as well as security personnel patrolling the property. Make sure the apartment has a working telephone, working air-conditioning, no water problems, and somewhere to park a car. Also check that any zapper you are given to open a security gate is fully functional. Noisy neighbors may be par for the course because loud music plays such an important part in the lives of Trinis. Check any contract carefully before you sign a lease. In Tobago, in particular, it may be possible to haggle over the price, particularly if you intend to stay for more than two weeks.

HEALTH

The level of health care for ordinary people is poor. There is public provision, but waiting times are long and there are not enough facilities. Folk medicine is becoming increasingly popular and street traders are to be found selling all sorts of remedies: local herb tonics, and other medicines with both Indian and African roots. Private health care is very expensive.

The islands have a network of public hospitals, health centers, and community clinics. Treatment is free to residents and nonresidents alike but expect to wait a long time before being attended to. Regional hospitals are not as well equipped as those in Port of Spain and medical personnel are prone to striking. There are a number of modern private hospitals, but proof of ability to pay is often required before treatment is given, even in emergencies. Medical insurance is therefore advised, including provision for evacuation.

Bring adequate supplies of prescription medicines. Common remedies can be bought over the counter at pharmacies in the major towns. They are normally open from 8:00 a.m. to 9:00 p.m. or 10:00 p.m., except on Sundays and public holidays.

Tobago's health care system and facilities are very limited. Treatment for minor ailments is available, but serious medical cases are referred to Trinidad. Tobago has a recompression facility for divers based at the Roxborough Medical Clinic on the northeast of the island.

Some Hazards and Precautions
The islands have a high prevalence of HIV/AIDS and there is a huge stigma around this issue. The government provides free AIDS medication and

treatment and there is an awareness campaign, but there are still many people who would rather die from AIDS than walk through the doors of a clinic, thereby letting it be known they are HIV positive.

Stray dogs are an all too common sight in Trinidad, and there has been a rise in the incidence of rabies among cats and cattle as well as dogs, so it is advisable not to pet any stray animal.

There are no venomous snakes in Tobago, but Trinidad has four, including coral snakes and two species of mapepire, all of which should be studiously avoided and looked out for when hiking in the bush. Wear long trousers for lengthy bush treks and never wear open-toed sandals. Snake bites and scorpion stings are, however, rare.

Once in Trinidad and Tobago, there is little risk to health other than the effects of too much sun or rum and bites from mosquitoes and sand flies. Sunscreen, sunglasses, and a hat are essential, as is insect repellent, particularly during the wet season.

The biggest natural dangers in T&T are the seasonal Portuguese Man O'War jellyfish, and the Manchineel tree. Man O'War infest the coastline and can be a hazard on the beach and in shallow waters. They are not true jellyfish but small, translucent air bladders with a purple or light blue hue. Once the tentacles make contact with the skin, they leave a very nasty sting. Rubbing or rinsing with water will make it worse. Flush or soak the area with vinegar for about thirty minutes, apply a 1 percent hydrocortisone cream, and get medical attention

The Manchineel is a medium-sized tree that grows at beaches and bears small green "apples" that attack the nervous system if they are bitten. Its leaves also exude a sap-like substance that blisters your skin. So it's wise to seek local advice as to whether these trees are present before you go onto a beach and in no circumstances shelter under a Manchineel tree when it rains. Avoid any sort of contact with the tree or its fruit.

Tap water is generally safe to drink but it is safest to boil and/or filter it first or simply drink bottled water, which is widely available in supermarkets, bars, local shops, and food stalls.

Salad needs to be thoroughly washed in boiled water. If buying sandwiches on the street, ask for them without salad.

Trinidad and Tobago has no malaria but there are periodic outbreaks of dengue fever.

Officially no specific shots are required, but visitors would be wise to check that no vaccines, mandatory immunizations, or special precautions are needed before their visit. A yellow fever vaccination certificate is, however, required for entry for people arriving in T&T within five days of leaving an area with yellow fever.

SAFETY
Terrorism

The Trinidad authorities have not forgotten that, in July 1990, an extremist Black Muslim group called the Jamaat al Muslimeen bombed the police station in Port of Spain and stormed the Red House, Trinidad's seat of government, following an unresolved grievance over land claims. The prime minister of the day and members of parliament were held hostage for five days, while panic, rioting, and looting spread through Port of Spain. After a lengthy standoff with the police and military, Jamaat leader Yasin Abu Bakr and his followers surrendered, having secured an amnesty. More than twenty people died during the attempted coup, including the member of parliament for Diego Martin Central. The hundred and fourteen members of the group were tried for treason and murder, but were released when the Court of Appeal upheld the amnesty. Many of them, including Abu Bakr, are still living in Trinidad.

In 2005, twelve people were injured when a bomb was detonated in front of the popular Smokey and Bunty bar in the heart of Port of Spain. It was the fourth bomb in Trinidad in three months but it was unclear who was responsible. The United States believes that a resurgent Jamaat al Muslimeen continues to be a threat to stability and the FBI has recently opened an office in Trinidad. In addition, an antiterrorism team has been established within the Special Anti-Crime Unit of Trinidad and Tobago to help enforce legislation passed in January 2010, which makes the funding of acts of terror a crime. It includes twenty-five-year prison sentences for anyone found guilty of financing terrorism.

There is no national service in Trinidad and Tobago, and visitors should be aware that it is illegal to wear military or camouflage clothing. Anyone so dressed risks being detained by customs officials and having the garments confiscated.

Crime

Trinidad has a huge problem with crime and shows little sign of coming to grips with it. There were 509 murders in 2009 and 550 in 2008. This constitutes a rate of 55 murders per 100,000 people, which makes it the most dangerous country in the Caribbean and one of the most dangerous in the world. Inadequate police numbers and training, lax detection of guns coming into the country, and drug running all contribute to this state of affairs.

The number of kidnappings for ransom has soared too, totaling 247 in the last five years. Incidents of assault, robbery, and rape in Trinidad and Tobago are also among the highest in the world. For law-abiding Trinis as well as visitors, these are depressing statistics.

In 2005 the Trinidad and Tobago Manufacturers Association, which represents some four hundred businesses, were so alarmed that they took out advertisements in newspapers accusing the government of failing to tackle crime. "Regardless of colour, creed, race or economic standing, we all live in constant fear of being robbed, kidnapped or killed. We no longer have a peaceful way of life," the TTMA said. Nothing much has changed since.

Much of the crime in Trinidad is gun and/or drug related and involves gangs. Money from drug trafficking is used to buy weapons and ammunition that are then used by feuding gangs, particularly in the tightly populated urban hillside areas such as Laventille and Morvant on the east side of Port of Spain's business district. These areas suffer greatly from the loss of their young men to gangs and drug wars, but the people of these poor communities somehow manage to retain a generosity of spirit. There is often understanding and sympathy for a young man who finds himself irretrievably trapped in a drug gang.

Gun-related homicides have increased tenfold in the last ten years and fewer than a fifth of crimes are ever solved. Some campaigners for a safer country, and even some members of the government, allege that police corruption is part of the problem, coupled with the reluctance of officers to come down hard on colleagues who profit from crime. This has resulted in the public placing little confidence in the police. There is a crime hotline, but some are afraid to use it, fearing their details will be passed on to the criminals.

For tourists, Tobago was always considered by far the safer of the two islands, but in recent years visitors have increasingly become victims of assault, robbery, and even murder. Private villas, particularly in the southwest of the island, have experienced violent robberies, and some visitors have even hired security officers. Steps have recently been taken to speed up investigations into crime involving tourists.

The proliferation of crime has led to both the USA and the UK issuing advisory notices warning travelers about increasing violence, the weakness of law enforcement, and the failure of police in Tobago to apprehend and prosecute criminals. One particular warning highlights the penchant for gangs to tail unsuspecting visitors from Piarco Airport in Trinidad only to assault and rob them in some quieter location or at their destination. Late night travel from Trinidad's Piarco Airport on the Beetham/Churchill Highway is to be avoided and extra vigilance should be taken on the Lady Young Road, an alternative airport route close to Port of Spain, where there have been instances of attempts to erect illegal traffic blocks.

In towns, grilles over windows and external lighting are common home security measures, and gated communities with patrolling uniformed guards are commonplace.

Common sense and vigilance are paramount for visitors. While driving at night in towns, car doors should be locked and windows rolled up. Similar safety precautions are advisable during the day in downtown Port of Spain. It is best to park in parking garages with an attendant if possible. Be extra careful when you return to your car that there is no one suspicious nearby aiming to jump in. Carry only the cash you need, avoid wearing flashy jewelry, and store valuables in hotel safety deposit boxes.

Drugs
Visitors need to be aware that there are several penalties, including long jail sentences, for possession and trafficking of illegal drugs.

Women and Harassment
Trinidad is not first and foremost a tourist island and foreign women are generally accepted as being a natural part of the community. Because they are neither a rarity nor a novelty, they do not automatically stand out, particularly in the big towns. They are usually capably independent, do not attract undue male attention when they are on their own, and are unlikely to be subjected to harassment. Any unwanted male approach can usually be quickly deflected by plain speaking or a clear indication of lack of interest.

Foreign women will, however, find themselves objects of male interest if they dress in beach clothes in towns and villages. The rule is to cover up and remember to respect the locals—their view is that you are in their town, their village, and should behave accordingly. Harassment rarely occurs at tourist resorts in Trinidad, where people are used to sharing the beaches with foreigners. It is important to note that topless or nude bathing is strictly forbidden.

In Tobago, the attitude to foreign women is very different. There are single white women who visit the island with the specific aim of finding themselves a man for a romantic holiday fling. Tobagonian men are well aware of this and so foreign women are much more likely to be approached than in Trinidad. Single foreign women are regarded as legitimate targets and friendly conduct will be interpreted as flirtation. Thus it is important to register your lack of interest at the very start of an unwanted advance. Once engaged in conversation, the man approaching you will very likely be persistent. "Not looking for man" is usually the effective Trini parlance to get the message across plainly. As in Trinidad, the dress rule is to cover up away from beaches, resorts, and swimming pools to avoid unwanted attention. Abiding by these commonsense rules will help to minimize, but not always eliminate, harassment.

chapter eight

BUSINESS BRIEFING

THE ECONOMIC CLIMATE

Trinidad and Tobago has had a booming economy driven by real GDP growth of 8 percent over the last decade and is the most diversified and industrialized economy in the English-speaking Caribbean. With proven reserves of petroleum and natural gas, and heavy industries such as iron and steel, methanol, and nitrogenous fertilizers well developed, it is committed to an open, market-driven economy with the encouragement of private enterprise and foreign investment. It has export market access to the United States, the European Union, Canada, and numerous other nations via special agreements. Among more than 150 international companies who have already established bases of operation in Trinidad and Tobago are high-profile firms such as BP, Amoco, Citicorp, Coca-Cola, Fujitsu, Johnson & Johnson, British Gas, Unilever, and PriceWaterhouseCoopers.

Government-owned institutions still exist and, because the civil service has proved less than totally efficient, the government has formed a number of "special purpose" state-owned companies to manage various projects. There have been nearly twenty such enterprises set up by the three administrations of prime minister Patrick Manning since the early 1990s. They range from a company managing the delivery and implementation of assigned infrastructure projects in the areas of drainage and flood control, highways and transportation, to a company formed to protect the country's intellectual property rights, inclusive of its patents, for the various forms of the country's official musical instrument—the pan.

The services sector is the largest in the economy, contributing on average $TT43 billion ($US6.8 billion) to GDP annually. It covers business services (professional, computer, and so on), construction, transport, communications, financial services, tourism, and travel, as well as government operations among others. This sector employs around 80 percent of the labor force.

The food and beverage industry is currently the largest in the nonmanufacturing sector, employing more than 9,000 people, which

contributes to a significant reduction of the country's food import bill. Back in the 1970s the government supported a drive to substitute foreign products with locally manufactured items. And, by 1993, after the liberalization of T&T's foreign exchange system, the range of products produced locally expanded considerably in response to competition. The food and beverage sector now has internationally recognized brands as well as many smaller companies specializing in Caribbean-based niche products.

As the leading Caribbean producer of oil and gas, Trinidad and Tobago maintains a buoyant economic climate with low inflation and likes to promote itself as an excellent site for international business. Proven success in the energy sector and a commitment to growth has created a solid business environment for foreign investment. This is actively encouraged by the government in the following marketplaces: petrochemicals, fish and fish processing, food and beverage,

information communications technology, leisure marine, and merchant marine.

The government recently launched major initiatives in the agriculture sector to bring a minimum additional 20,000 acres (8,094 ha) of land into production by 2012. It also introduced a strategy of highly organized large farm development, having recognized that T&T's agricultural sector is dominated by small, disorganized, low technology farmers.

For foreigners, unless their business requires a license for mining or drilling, leasing government-owned land, or getting tax concessions, it is possible to invest without too much red tape. Foreigner businesspeople find that a local partner can help cut through a lot of the red tape.

Anyone wishing to incorporate a company in T&T is required by law to register the business. Limited liability companies can enjoy a tax credit of 25 percent of their taxable profits by attaining Approved Small Company status through the Business Development Company Ltd.

T&T is regarded as the financial center of the Caribbean. Major banks there include Republic Bank Limited, Royal Bank of Trinidad and Tobago Limited, Scotiabank Trinidad and Tobago Limited, and First Citizens Bank.

THE BUSINESS LANDSCAPE

It's really only Port of Spain, and to a lesser extent Scarborough in Tobago, which have excellent business facilities. The major hotels have modern business centers fully equipped with satellite television, fax, printing facilities, and wireless Internet connections. A thriving financial sector, a burgeoning manufacturing industry, and a proven energy sector means that Trinidad's major hotel chains operate at near capacity with business travelers all year-round.

Whereas traditional management style in T&T used to be from the top down, these days team management is increasingly common, with middle management very much involved. Foreigners will find the pace of business much slower than in the USA and Europe, and that it will take time to create networks and establish personal relationships. But it is worth making the time and effort to network, as good personal relationships and connections are just as important as in British or American companies.

Foreign businesspeople who find the more leisurely "Trini time" frustrating should simply adjust to the pace. Patience is the name of the game. Trinis rarely understand a need to hurry.

Both the government sector and private businesses work a five-day week Monday to Friday, although some of the latter work on Saturday. Business hours are generally from 8:00 a.m. to 4:00 p.m., although smaller businesses tend to start later and may stay open as late as 8:00 p.m. Many government offices close at 4:00 p.m. Banking hours are generally from 8:00 a.m. to 2:00 p.m. Monday to Thursday. On Fridays, banks open from 8:00 a.m. to 12 noon, then resume at 3:00 p.m. until 5:00 p.m. Banks located in shopping plazas and malls are an exception and are open continuously from 10:00 a.m. to 5:00 p.m. All banks have ABMs and shopping malls contain either full service branches or ABMs. Traveler's checks and credit cards are accepted in most establishments, but the Customs and Excise division accepts cash only.

Trade unions are strong and independent, and the government doesn't exercise tight control over them. Although there have been difficult times in the past, labor relations are currently stable.

BUSINESS ETIQUETTE
Formality and Respect
Trinis who have titles such as Doctor like to be addressed appropriately, and when writing to someone in a business communication, the polite prefix "The right honorable" is used. In a country of such multiethnicity, it's important to take care to spell names correctly. Failure to observe these fundamental niceties may be construed as arrogance, a trait in foreigners that Trinis will resent strongly.

Business Cards
Business cards are essential, to be exchanged at every opportunity. They can be printed very quickly and cheaply in the main towns. Business cards you receive from contacts should be studied carefully to make sure you address your contact correctly.

Dress

Men are expected to wear light business suits and ties to formal or first meetings. Jackets and ties are acceptable at informal meetings. Jeans and T shirts are never acceptable, however hot and humid the weather may be. Wearing any jewelry other than a wedding ring may be considered unprofessional. In Tobago, jackets are optional except on formal occasions. Women should dress conservatively in a business context. Figure-hugging outfits or low necklines are to be avoided, and skirts should be modest with hems below the knee when sitting down. Pantsuits are an acceptable and popular option.

When "Trini Time" Does Not Apply

While Trinidad and Tobago enjoys a laid-back, unhurried pace of life, it's important to note that business appointments generally run on time. Foreigners are expected to be punctual. If you are running behind, it is polite to notify your contact by phone that you will be late. Allow plenty of time to get to your meeting because traffic congestion or a road accident can cause long delays, especially during the rush hour.

MEETINGS

The first approach is best done by telephone or by e-mail. After arranging a mutually convenient day and time to meet in advance, it is worth confirming this with your contact's secretary nearer the date. First meetings will be very formal affairs. If it is a one-to-one meeting, it will most likely be held in the place of business. But with the growing trend toward working in teams, the meeting may well take place at a business center or in a conference room at one of the major hotels.

Punctuality is important. Meetings tend to start off with a little small talk before getting down to business, but religion and politics are topics to be avoided. Once the meeting is underway it's advisable to stick to the matter in hand without diversions into stories or jokes. A formal agenda will be adhered to, and you are unlikely to be interrupted by phone calls, people coming in with papers to sign, or trays of drinks. After the meeting has broken up, it's acceptable and polite to engage in a little social chat before leaving.

Presentations
It is best to make clear at the start how long your presentation will take and to use that time accordingly. A mixture of straightforward but not overly detailed information, visual aids, and the occasional slice of humor will go down well. If

you are interrupted, don't let this faze you, but in any case leave time for questions at the end.

Do not be offended by any late arrivals, though this is less likely to happen the higher up your audience.

Negotiations
The Trinbagonian negotiation style is generally direct, open, and maybe tinged with a little humor. Try to ensure that you end up dealing with someone who is on at least the same level of importance as you, or who is a decision maker.

Leave enough room for discussion. When it comes to price Trinis prefer to cut to the chase and avoid having to negotiate down to the bottom line. Negotiating with government bodies is less straightforward as they sometimes have hidden agendas, either politically or historically, or ulterior motives, whereas business in the private sector is usually driven directly by profit and loss.

CONTRACTS
Trinidad and Tobago has a sound legal system based on English common law, and contracts are respected. Contracts will be in English and once signed are legally binding. Even so, to ensure smooth fulfillment it's a good idea to keep the relationship going in a balanced way. There will be clauses in any contract covering disagreements and the way they should be handled. Disputes are settled in court. Trinis are not particularly litigious and, if a dispute goes to court, the courts

are effective and fair, but the process is often frustratingly slow.

If you are managing staff in a T&T company, the wisest way of handling a dispute is to find out all the facts by letting people have their say and then to negotiate—and, importantly, to be seen to negotiate—in a fair and proper manner.

DEALING WITH THE GOVERNMENT

It is essential to seek professional advice when dealing with the government in order to keep abreast of the latest rules and regulations. A number of permits and licenses may be required before business can proceed, and there are several government Web sites that contain up-to-date information. There is considerable lack of transparency in government institutions, leading to the possibility of corruption. You can be subject to arbitrary decisions at any stage before a contract is signed, and you may suddenly be given a veto from the top.

CORRUPTION

Trinis grow up with corruption on an everyday basis. There are common instances, ranging from payments to facilitate clearance of goods at ports, to getting building plans approved, or the

installation of water connections by the water authority. Even the chairman of the TT Transparency Institute described Trinidad and Tobago in 2010 as "a society of corruption" after the islands ranked 72 out of 180 countries in the annual Global Corruption Report of Transparency International.

The widespread petty corruption fuels and encourages grand corruption. For evidence, Trinis know they need look no further than the scandal of Trinidad's TT$1.6 billion (US$256.2 million) Piarco Airport Development Project. An inquiry into allegations of massive fraud and conspiracy by contractors at the Airports Authority, and by others, has been going on for no less than seven years and is a sore that continues to fester.

High-level corruption is openly discussed in the local media, which have a good record of exposing bribery and corruption in the government's house-building program and other construction projects. The government, for its part, makes sporadic attempts to clean itself up and in 2010 set up the Trinidad and Tobago Revenue Authority to stamp out widespread corruption within the Board of Inland Revenue and Customs and Excise. Bribery is rare in the private sector.

BUSINESS GIFTS

Legitimate business gifts are not uncommon and are usually exchanged at the end of the year. A small token such as a souvenir from one's own country rather than an obvious sweetener is acceptable as a first time gift. Gifts are a goodwill gesture toward contacts with whom you have developed a professional relationship or wish to do so. Keep the gift simple and inexpensive; otherwise your contact will feel pressured into reciprocating with a gift of the same value.

WOMEN IN BUSINESS

Women in executive positions are taken very seriously and expect to be treated as equals. The number of women in senior positions in T&T is increasing: there have now been several generations of well educated Indian women who have not been pressured into first and foremost becoming a homemaker. Rather than following the traditional life path of staying at home and helping out in a small family business, many women are now independent high achievers, aspiring to more ambitious positions in the wider business world.

In 2010 the chairperson of the T&T Chamber of Commerce was a woman, but it is still unusual to find a woman as the final decision-maker in a big company. Any sign of intimacy toward a woman in business matters should be strictly avoided. Inviting a female contact out to lunch is acceptable and will not be taken as any sort of a romantic overture, but an invitation to dinner is a step too far in a business context. Business lunches generally should take no more than two hours.

chapter nine

COMMUNICATING

LANGUAGE

English is the official language and is
spoken throughout the islands. But
there are some parts of Trinidad
where Spanish is still spoken and,
by being taught in schools, it is
being promoted as Trinidad and
Tobago's first foreign language.
Many of Trinidad's folk songs are in
Spanish, and the islands play host to a
number of visitors from neighboring Venezuela.
In addition, some French patois is common, and
Hindi and Urdu are spoken in Indian
communities.

Although standard English is the prime
language, the language of education and choice,
Trinidad has its own unique colloquialisms, its
own slang made up of words and inflections from
each nationality that has ruled, visited, and lived
there. Trinis will tell you that the only two words
you need to understand are "fete" and "lime." The
former, we have seen, is the major-sized party
featuring very loud music, dancing, good food,
and lots of drink, which makes for "plenty

bacchanal," while the lime is more of a casual meeting of friends for the purpose of not doing very much in particular. The verb "to lime" means to hang out with friends and family, to pass the time, and to chill out.

Tobagonians also use a local Creole dialect that is a mix of patois and derivations of French, Dutch, and Amerindian, and, while many of the Trini words and pet phrases are pidgin English with a Spanish or French flavor, some are not as self-explanatory or as easily guessed as "Yeah Oui" meaning yes or "Tanty" for auntie.

Trinidad and Tobago's unique dialect cuts across anything taught in school pertaining to grammar: words are shortened or expanded, singular is mixed with plural, the past tense blurred with the present (such as "we reach" for "we have arrived.") And the simplest slang is derived from the omission or substitution of letters such as "dat" for that, "ting" for thing, and "t'ree" for three. Nouns and verbs are also frequently turned upside down, as in "fire de work," meaning chucking in one's job.

A tale told in the colorful Trini dialect is often embroidered with a "speaking with the hands"— the kind of flamboyant gesticulation employed by a traffic cop on duty at a faulty traffic light at rush hour.

The best way to learn to "talk de talk" of Trinidad and Tobago and to understand it is to immerse yourself in the society and to read the newspapers. Any foreigner who wants to spend a long time in T&T would do well to seek out the *Trinidad and Tobago Dictionary*, compiled specifically for visitors.

TRINBAGONIAN ENGLISH

Catchin' yuh tail Down on your luck, without money

Doogla A person of mixed race

Fedupsy Bored

Fire one Take a drink, as in "fire one fo d road"

Fresh water Yankee Someone who spends a short time in the USA and returns with an American accent

Fruit doh fall far from d tree Children are rarely different from their parents

Hol' strain Wait a moment

Make style To show off

Ramcram Packed to capacity

Upstairs house Two-story dwelling

Vampin' Offensive smell, as in "dat vampin' man" who smells really bad

Yuh business fix You're all organized now

Zeppo A hot tip, or gossip whispered in secret

BODY LANGUAGE

The unhurried pace of life in the islands is reflected in the leisurely gait of the locals. African Trinbagonians are more tactile and demonstrative than the Indians and the difference is especially noticeable at fetes, where their dancing is less inhibited, and at sporting events, where African Trinis are much more expressive of their appreciation or disgust at the performance of their team. Similarly, in a social context and even in business, the African demeanor is more outgoing than that of the Indians, who have a certain reserve.

THE MEDIA

Newspapers are the main source of news and information. The press is free and there are no government-owned newspapers. Trinidad's main daily is the *Trinidad Guardian*, a serious but lively broadsheet. The other dailies are both tabloids, the *Trinidad Express* and the picture-led *Newsday*. All three publish expanded weekend editions to include TV schedules, lifestyle, home, music, and fashion features as well as sections for children. A range of down-market Sunday papers, including *Sunday Punch*, *The Mirror*, *Heat*, *Blast*, and *Bomb*, are hugely popular. They carry stories with

screaming headlines about shocking crimes, pictures of bikini-clad girls, and political exposés. There is only one daily newspaper in Tobago, the *Tobago News*, which is published every Friday and covers island events.

Local newspapers are sold at supermarkets, gas stations, pharmacies, and by vendors at busy road junctions in towns. Several major American magazines, such as *Cosmopolitan*, *Time*, *Style*, and *Newsweek*, are readily available but *USA Today* is generally the only foreign daily newspaper on sale. Local glossy magazines *Maco* and *She* feature upscale homes, fashion, and lifestyle and *Ins & Outs* and *Discover Trinidad & Tobago* are two highly informative magazines published annually covering all things Trinbagonian.

Radio is very popular and there are thirty FM and two AM stations, the majority of which pump out the kind of music for which the islands are famous. But they are also good at providing information about various events and celebrations.

Television stations range from the state-owned national station C to Gayelle, a privately owned local-oriented station. All the major hotels have satellite TV.

SERVICES
Telephone
Communication in Trinidad and Tobago has improved enormously in recent years and there is

now a modern infrastructure with the latest in digital technology and fiber-optic systems. The introduction of modern and efficient telephone systems means that it is easy to call virtually anywhere around the world. Almost everybody in T&T has relatives abroad with whom they want to keep in contact on a regular basis. The favored option of staying in touch is the use of Internet telephone, partly because it's cheaper. For directory inquiries dial 6411.

EMERGENCY PHONE NUMBERS

Police 999 or 555
Ambulance 990
Fire 990
Coastguard 634 4440

There are currently two cell phone networks in T&T—Digicel and Bmobile. Healthy competition between the two has made owning a cell phone comparatively inexpensive and consequently sales have soared. The social impact has been enormous, particularly among the young. Cell phones are all the more vital because pay phones are hard to find in towns and very rare in more rural areas, especially

in Tobago. Prepaid cards can be bought from local outlets, small grocery stores, and at lottery ticket stands. A sign on the door will usually indicate cards are for sale.

Mail

The postal system TTPost is at best unreliable and at worst extremely erratic. It is impossible to predict how long a letter or packet to or from Europe will take to arrive. A small percentage of letters and packets fail to reach their destination at all, so it is advisable to send anything important by registered mail via the Post Office or by foreign couriers. A number of private courier firms are in operation, including FedEx, DHL, G4, and Securicor, but are limited to a few towns.

Mailboxes are colored red. It is wisest to send mail from major towns, and probably quicker if posted in post offices and hotels. Packages are liable to be opened at customs if deemed to require duty payment. Stamps can be bought at post offices or hotels. Mail sent to you should bear your name, house or apartment number, street, area, town or city, Trinidad or Tobago, West Indies.

Internet

Access to the Internet is now widely available and has been expanding rapidly since the arrival of

cable broadband. There are some
Internet cafés in town areas but
they are very limited elsewhere.
In homes, anyone with a phone
line and a modem can
connect to the Internet,
either by subscribing to an
Internet Service Provider or by using one of the
free numbers. High-speed connections are the
norm in Internet cafés but not all have wireless.
Usually a café will display a sign if it has Wi-Fi.

CONCLUSION

Trinbagonians, for all their cultural and ethnic
diversity, share a fundamentally positive outlook.
Steeped in the religious values of their respective
beliefs, they are tolerant of other faiths and
nationalities. They are laid-back, warm, and
friendly, with a capacity for celebration that
manifests itself at every opportunity.

The typical Trini response to any sign of
impatience is to ask why there is a need to hurry.
Visitors may occasionally find this ultra-relaxed
and fatalistic attitude frustrating. For foreigners, a
shrug of the shoulders when things go wrong can
be exasperating, but for Trinis it is a tried and
trusted stress-free method of coping with setbacks
and problems. They are usually anxious to please,
though as we have seen this desire does not
necessarily translate into the action required.
Rather than disappoint, the tendency can be to do

nothing at all rather than something that might possibly be wrong. Personal pride means that they dislike showing any sort of ignorance, and their inclination is to pretend to know something when quizzed rather than admit any lack of knowledge. These foibles apart, Trinbagonians are outgoing, genuine, good-humored people who value strong relationships and friendships. Their life-affirming determination to enjoy themselves is infectious, and any visitor who is prepared to go with the flow will find acceptance. Trinidad legend has it that if on your visit you eat cascadoux you will return to the islands. Many do!

Further Reading

Anthony, Michael. *Profile Trinidad. A Historical Survey from the Discovery to 1900*. London: Macmillan Caribbean, 1974.

——— . *Towns and Villages of Trinidad and Tobago*. Marabella, Trinidad: Printmaster (W.I) Ltd, 2001.

——— . *Green Days by the River*. Oxford: Heinemann, 2000.

Anthony, Michael, and Andrew Carr. *David Frost Introduces Trinidad and Tobago*. London: Andre Deutsch, 1975.

Clarke, Colin, and Gillian Clarke. *Post-Colonial Trinidad: An Ethnographic Journal*. Basingstoke, Hampshire: Palgrave Macmillan, 2010.

Dudley, Shannon. *Music from behind the Bridge: Steelband Aesthetics and Politics in Trinidad and Tobago*. Oxford: Oxford University Press, 2007

Mason, Peter. *Bacchanal! The Carnival Culture of Trinidad*. Philadelphia: Temple University Press, 1999.

Mendes, John. *Cote Ci Cote La*. Trinidad: MediaNet Caribbean, 2004.

Naipaul, V.S. *The Mystic Masseur*. New York: Vintage Books, 2002.

———. *A House For Mr. Biswas*. London: Picador, 2003.

Ottley, C.R. *The Story of Tobago*. New Jersey: Prentice Hall Press, 1973.

Stuempfle, Stephen. *The Steelband Movement: The Forging of a National Art in Trinidad and Tobago*. Philadelphia PA: University of Pennsylvania Press, 1996.

Williams, Eric. *History of the People of Trinidad and Tobago*. New York: A& B Publishers Group, 1993.

culture smart! **trinidad and tobago**

Index

Acknowledgments

Grateful thanks for their help and cooperation to Peter Pasea and to
Carole Anne Ferris at www.cafemokagallery.com